Weaving a Library Web

A Guide to Developing Children's Websites

HELENE BLOWERS

ROBIN BRYAN

AMERICAN LIBRARY ASSOCIA

Chicago   2004

Composition by ALA Editions in ITC Legacy Sans and Galliard using Quark XPress 5.0 on a PC Platform

Printed on 50-pound white offset, a pH-neutral stock, and bound in 10-point coated cover stock by McNaughton & Gunn

The paper used in this publication meets the minimum requirements of American National Standard for Information Sciences—Permanence of Paper for Printed Library Materials, ANSI Z39.48-1992. ∞

Library of Congress Cataloging-in-Publication Data

Blowers, Helene.
    Weaving a library Web : a guide to developing children's websites / by Helene Blowers and Robin Bryan.
        p. cm.
    Includes bibliographical references and index.
    ISBN 0-8389-0877-2 (alk. paper)
    1. Internet in children's libraries. 2. Library Web sites—Design. 3. Children's Web sites—Design. I. Bryan, Robin. II. Title.
    Z718.1.B55 2004
    025.04—dc22   2004001806

Printed in the United States of America

08   07   06   05   04   5   4   3   2   1

CONTENTS

ILLUSTRATIONS

ACKNOWLEDGMENTS

The creation of this book could not have begun without the combined support and talents of so many people. Without their creativity, imagination, and collective abilities we would have nothing really to write about. To them we say a "big thanks" for making the creation of this book a reality.

To Robert Cannon, former Executive Director of the Public Library of Charlotte and Mecklenburg County (PLCMC). Thank you for your leadership and vision in developing library websites that help to push the envelope in reshaping remote library services.

To the Web Services Team of PLCMC. Thank you for your amazing skills and abilities in developing fresh new approaches, colorful engaging designs, and interactive elements, and for providing the programming backbone to make it all work so well.

To all the PLCMC website teams. Thank you for continuing to churn out great new ideas that help us reshape the public's perspective of what libraries can offer through the Web and for providing the support and energy to promote and maintain PLCMC's websites.

To our respective spouses, David Blowers and Donald Bryan. Thank you for putting up with our absences from family time during this book's development and for your ongoing support of our endeavors. We're both very lucky to have you in our corners.

INTRODUCTION

We have entered a digital age in which preschoolers can handle a mouse better than a crayon. In this digital world children want to interact with information, not just receive it. Technology is as ordinary to them as television and radio were to previous generations. Computers and the Internet provide them with information and entertainment, sometimes to the exclusion of all else. Where does the library fit into this digital picture? Can we compete with a gigabyte Goliath?

The solution is to fight technology with technology. Instead of fearing the Internet as a pied piper luring children away from books, libraries should embrace its possibilities. The Internet can become a tool to bring the library to children, and to bring children into the library. This can be accomplished by creating service websites for children that offer traditional library services such as readers' advisory and homework assistance that go beyond information by providing an empowering information environment. This book will provide you with insight into and guidance in planning and creating such sites.

This book is for children's librarians who wish to explore expanding their children's services via the Web. This is not a technical manual but a guide to the process of developing and implementing children's service websites. Anyone interested in developing quality, advertisement-free children's sites can benefit from this work. We have broken this guide into sections that deal with the planning process, design guidelines and special technical considerations, testing, marketing, and best practices, so you can read through the entire book or pinpoint the information that is most relevant to your project.

There are already several books about creating library service websites and guides on how to use the Internet to serve children. However, we believe that this book is the first to address the development of library service sites for children based on a team approach that can be adapted for use in both small and large libraries.

In writing this book, we wish to share the knowledge and experience we have gleaned from the development of the Public Library of Charlotte and Mecklenburg County's family of websites. Four of the thirteen sites that our library currently supports have been developed specifically for children: BookHive, StoryPlace, Brarydog, and Hands on Crafts. (For more information on our family of websites, visit http://www.plcmc.org.) Each of these sites has enjoyed great success in offering library services to children both locally and nationally, but this success has not come without failures and lessons learned. We feel fortunate to be part of a library system that has been in the forefront of developing Internet services for children, and as the many examples in this book show, several other libraries are joining the ranks. It is our hope that this book will encourage libraries to explore the possibilities and follow suit in finding ways to offer children's services online.

CHAPTER 1

Kids and the Internet

M ost of us can still remember the early days of the Internet, when its development methodology was rooted in a belief popularized by *Field of Dreams,* a 1988 movie about baseball that introduced the slogan "If you build it, they will come." During those early days everyone (businesses, not-for-profit associations, individuals, and, yes, even libraries) was busy trying to find some way to benefit from this new global communication tool. The emergence of the Internet and the proliferation of home computers in the early 1990s promised to level the playing field for organizations, both large and small, by giving them an equal ability to market their services and products to a mass public. You might even have called it a "cyberfield of dreams."

If the first decade of the World Wide Web explosion has taught us anything, it is that to survive in cyberspace, we need to build more than a mere web presence—we need to build a *web service.* In today's virtual climate, most libraries are already on the second, third, or even fourth generation of their library website. One reason behind so much change has been to keep up with the developments in technology, bandwidth, connection speed, and browser capabilities. But a greater reason can be attributed to the changes in our patrons' needs and perceptions. Patrons are demanding more from their libraries in regard to collections, program offerings, information, and remote-access services. The expansion of search indexes and web bots has also assisted library patrons in becoming more sophisticated seekers of information. With each successive generation of search tools (Yahoo, Google, and the like), users have become more accomplished in locating information for themselves. Granted, the amount of material a user must wade through before finding relevant information may have increased, but that is more likely due to the overwhelming volume of information available on the Web than to an individual's search savviness. Today's library patrons are smarter, more sophisticated researchers (at least when it comes to the Web) and more demanding in their informational expectations and needs. No longer are they content to wait two weeks for an interlibrary loan title to come in. They want immediate access to resources that can provide the information they need and tools that will enable them to locate the information themselves. Libraries meet these new demands and challenges not only by continuing to develop real-time solutions that provide access to traditional library services (such as reference and readers' advisory) but also, more importantly, *by redefining how they offer service.* To do this, libraries must reinvent themselves as *developers* of information and lifelong-learning services rather than continuing to act as mere providers.

To appeal to our youngest library users, the importance of stepping up to this challenge is significant. Nowadays, many children learn to use a computer mouse before they can read a book. They can manipulate images and text on a screen before they can write their names. They have no understanding of what life was like before the personal computer (PC). To today's generation, computers and digital technology go hand in hand with learning, information, and knowledge. To reach these young patrons, we must adapt and reinvent many of our core children's library services so that they relate to the technology-driven learning environment that children are growing up in. For children's libraries this means taking a fundamental look at what we currently do—and have always done—best for children and finding new ways to reach kids through the communication and educational channels they are comfortable with. It is only by reaching out to children in their world through the tools they are familiar with that we can best hope to stimulate their love of books, knowledge, and reading. Be assured that we are not advocating that libraries completely abandon over a hundred years of traditional children's library services in an effort to build new technology-driven ones. We all know that parents, caregivers, and our communities would instantly rise up and protest at the mere suggestion that we would try to replace a successful story-hour program with a new library website. Nor can we imagine a children's library without books, programs, and story hours. They are the bricks and mortar of any library's service offerings for children and the foundation for building a child's imagination, creativity, and literacy. Our physical library structures are still vitally important to our communities, not just because they provide access to books and materials, but also because they provide an enriched learning environment that empowers a young child to become a lifelong learner and a contributing member of society. To do this well, we must continually seek new ways to capture the attention of future generations and bridge the gap between our world and their world.

OUR WORLD

As librarians and children's specialists, we should already have a good idea of what our libraries do well. We know that libraries

Excel in promoting reading and literacy

Provide excellence in building collections (print, media, electronic, and the like) that meet children's interests and needs on a variety of reading levels

Foster self-sufficient learning by offering children guidance and assistance with information

Support our communities and the needs of teachers, parents, and caregivers who nurture children directly

And we know that the programming offered within our libraries (such as storytelling, bilingual offerings, and homework assistance) reach children in our communities on many levels, engaging them in imaginative activities that help promote the love of reading, learning, and life.

The introduction of the Internet has not really changed any of this. In fact, if you do a quick Internet search of libraries' mission statements, you will find that the core elements of many mission statements are pretty much the same from library to library and reflect what we do best. The main differences between most mission statements of the early 1990s and those of today stem from the introduction of technology. Many public library statements today include some type of declaration regarding access to electronic information and integration of new technologies into services. This is fairly common. What is not as common is the acknowledgment of how the introduction of the Internet and the World Wide Web has changed who we provide services to—our definition of community. Most libraries still recognize themselves as providing services to only their local patron population, not taking into account the global reach that they might actually have. Only a handful of institutions seem to actually grasp the impact the Internet has had on their user base. These libraries realize what our young users already know—that information can come from anywhere, that there are no community boundaries when it comes to locating (or providing) quality resources, and that there are fewer and fewer physical limitations to accessing it.

Here are some examples of public library mission statements that address the global impact that the Internet has had in providing service to their communities:

> The Ohio County Public Library . . . exists to provide books and related materials that will assist the residents of the community in the pursuit of knowledge, information, education, research, and recreation in order to promote an enlightened citizenry and to enrich their quality of life. The library will seek to fulfill this mission by . . . providing access to optimum information systems and services on a local, national, and global level.[1]
> —Ohio County Public Library System, Wheeling, West Virginia

> Our mission is to become the best public library in the world by being so tuned in to the people we serve and so supportive of each other's efforts that we are able to provide highly responsive service. We strive to inform, enrich and empower every person in our community by creating and promoting easy access to a vast array of ideas and information, and by supporting an informed citizenry, lifelong learning and love of reading. We acquire, organize and provide books and other relevant materials; ensure access to information sources throughout the nation and around the world; serve our public with expert and caring assistance; and reach out to all members of our community.[2]　　　　　—Seattle Public Library, Seattle, Washington

In addition to acknowledging the impact that Internet and electronic technologies have had when it comes to servicing their communities, a few libraries (including the public library we work for) have also developed separate mission statements for their websites that address their library's impact on its definition of community.

> The mission of the Public Library of Charlotte and Mecklenburg County's website (http://www.plcmc.org) is to provide residents of Mecklenburg

County and *potential users around the world* with a user friendly gateway to reviewed informational resources on the Internet, information about PLCMC's services, programs and collections, and direct access to on-line resources and PLCMC services.[3] —Public Library of Charlotte and Mecklenburg County, Charlotte, North Carolina

Once the question of who is affected by the Internet is addressed, the next question is how the Internet has changed what we, as children's libraries, do well. In preparation for this discussion we posted several questions on the Association for Library Service to Children (ALSC) and Public Libraries, Young Adults, and Children (PUBYAC) Listservs during the fall of 2002. In our survey, we asked children's librarians throughout the country to tell us how the World Wide Web has changed the way that they offer or provide library services to children. In particular, we asked the following:

How has the Internet changed the way you provide readers' advisory to youth?

How has the Internet altered the way you provide homework assistance/reference help?

What impact has the WWW had on your children's programs and what you offer?

Have your outreach services changed any as a result of this technology?

It was not surprising to find that answers to these questions varied greatly from the definitive "it hasn't changed anything" to "it's impacted all [our] services." Despite such extreme differences in opinion, the overwhelming number of responses did indicate that the introduction of the Internet has created a positive change in how services are provided. As one librarian summed it up, the Internet allows us, as libraries, to reach out to children by providing "the multimedia experience. Now youth who can process information better with visuals, etc., are not left in the dust [and] the ability to explore subjects with one click . . . allows eager minds to explore."

By exploring the "how" as it relates to children's libraries, we can not only discover what types of Internet services are of value to children but also, more importantly, identify the types of services that are provided best by libraries and that might be candidates for new Internet projects. To assist in this exploration, we will look at how many libraries are using the Internet today to offer traditional children's services.

Readers' Advisory

"A good book is still a good book" one children's librarian replied, and "a well-read librarian is still the way to go." No one can argue with that statement—nor should they. However, the technologies that the Internet has introduced allow us to become more well read, more knowledgeable, and more able to assist patrons. How many times has a young patron or adult approached you looking for a rare title, an unusual subject area, or an obscure book series? For years Novelist was the only electronic tool available for libraries and patrons to use when researching such requests. Now in addition, many library staff consult Amazon.com or Barnes and Noble Online because of their sophisticated database structures and user-preference-intelligent software. Those sites provide not only a book's synopsis and professional journal reviews, but also reviews, comments, and recommendations from readers—ordinary people who just like to read. As another survey participant put it, "Nothing beats Amazon's personalization features. Their new book e-mail service keeps me notified of new titles and also provides reviews." Many children's libraries have taken this concept further by creating their own web pages that offer book recommendations from staff, links to useful sites, and author pages. Another respondent noted, "We use the web to create reading lists and recommendations for children through our kids pages. Parents love it and it helps us direct them to appropriate suggestions for their child." Simply put, the Internet has enhanced children's readers' advisory by serving as a strong support tool for recommending good books to read.

Homework Assistance and Reference Help

Without a doubt the Internet has provided a springboard for many libraries in their attempts to provide students with homework assistance. Almost every children's librarian across the country can easily identify at least one yearly local school assignment that, without the benefit of the Internet, would cripple the library's ability to serve. "The Internet is a godsend for small branches, where we run out of [materials on], say, grasslands and prairies after the fourth child from class comes in to our branch," notes one survey participant. "There are some days, I can't imagine how we ever got by without it." Of course, she is also quick to point out that what she "really enjoy[s] is gently placing a print resource next to a child searching the Internet for a school assignment and who has spent a frustrating 20 minutes or so of finding nothing—Oh, the look on their faces!" I am sure we all can attest to similar experiences, because the Internet can be both a blessing and an aggravation. On one hand, it provides access to a never-ending and constantly growing wealth of information and gives libraries the means to expand their knowledge collection without budgetary consequences. On the other hand, it often slows students' progress in locating quality information resources and in some cases encourages an intolerance of printed materials. However, no matter which side of the debate you find yourself leaning toward, the Internet provides one benefit that most of us can agree on: the Internet, and the frustrations it can sometimes bring, often gives us the opportunity to share with young people that "ah-ha!" eye-opening experience about the power of books—the true foundation of all libraries.

In the last decade, many children's libraries have vastly expanded their use of the Internet and electronic resources to develop tools that support homework requests. "In several of our library's regional locations," notes one survey participant, "we routinely create web pages that provide pathfinders and subject guides for common school assignments" that can be accessed by students and staff. These pages are often placed on the library's website or intranet so that everyone can benefit from the staff's global expertise. Additionally, some libraries have taken it upon themselves to fill gaps by creating homework-supporting content for students when no quality print or electronic resources are available. One example of this is the Public Library of Charlotte and Mecklenburg County's history site titled the Charlotte-Mecklenburg Story (http://www.cmstory.org). Not only is this site rich in local history information, archives, and images that are helpful for school assignments, but in addition students have access to a publication created just for them, "A Student's Guide to Government and Officials." This staff-created publication addresses fourth-grade school assignments and has become a valuable resource for the library's numerous branches and smaller locations.

Programming

In many public libraries, programming appears to be the area of children's services least affected by the introduction of technology and the Internet—at least so far. And this is not surprising given the popularity of story times. Some might say that story times are the greatest legacy that children's services provide because they introduce young minds to new experiences that nurture the imagination and foster lifelong enjoyment of books and reading. But many libraries these days are offering much more in the way of programs that strongly support upper-elementary and middle-school students. In addition, the increase in home schooling in recent years along with the national movement to reach out to teens and preteens have prompted libraries to expand their program offerings. Many of those programs have tackled such topics as finding information on the Internet, developing searching skills, and even basic website design.

At the Burlington County Library in Westampton, New Jersey, children aged seven years and up can participate in a Cyber Surfer's Internet Scavenger Hunt that helps them develop savvy searching and online research skills. And the Providence Public Library in Providence, Rhode Island, takes children's technology programming a step further by offering year-round after-school and Saturday-morning Whiz Kids programs (http://www.provlib.org/kids/kids.htm). Students in grades 5 through 8 can participate in a variety of four- or six-week programs covering such computer literacy topics as computer hardware, designing a flyer in MS Word, creating a PowerPoint slide show, and even learning HTML basics and creating digital movies. In the library's junior program, for grades 3 and 4, activities are strongly tied to books. After children share in a read-aloud story with a group, they are encouraged to complete an activity on the computer (for example, a word search or crossword puzzle) that supports the story they just heard. "For all our activities, we try to keep in mind that this is after school and kids need to have fun," explains Gloria Church, the Whiz Kids Program Coordinator. These two examples are only the tip of the iceberg. In countless settings across the country, librarians are using the Internet to locate tested and successful program ideas, take-home activities, and reading lists that support their in-library programming. "There must be hundreds, if not thousands of websites about programming for children," notes one survey respondent. "If I need a song, a tune, or a craft idea, I can easily go online and find what I need."

Outreach Services

For many libraries around the country children's outreach services entail delivering story-time sessions at sites outside the physical library. And, indeed, this type of service is as fundamental to children's outreach as in-house story times are to children's programming. When we first compiled our survey, we were not sure what responses we might get from children's librarians to a question about how the Internet has influenced the outreach services they provide. For the most part, the responses indicated that there was little or no effect beyond providing another means of communicating with day-care facilities and other suppliers of child care. And then we received a response from one children's specialist that both surprised and thrilled us. "Technology has enabled libraries to expand their offerings beyond the physical walls and has allowed us to redefine 'outreach services.' It's not just about packing a bag full of books and music and heading out into the community. Now it encompasses developing websites that allow patrons to have a 'library experience' at home." Clearly this was a different way of looking at outreach services and a definition that encourages us to think outside the box. If this book accomplishes one thing, we hope that it is to prompt you to think about your library's Internet services in this new way. We all need to look at Internet services not merely as mechanisms that inform patrons about events and information found within children's libraries but rather as outreach vehicles that expand our libraries into the lives and world of our users—children.

THEIR WORLD

In doing research for this chapter, we came across an interesting site, The Shifted Librarian (http://theshiftedlibrarian.com), that poignantly hits upon one of the greatest challenges that libraries face as they begin to reinvent themselves for today's younger Net generation. This challenge is rooted in the fundamental reality that young "people aren't going out to get information anymore. Instead, it's coming to them."

"If you're around kids at all today, you can easily see how differently they think and act about information and technology. . . . The biggest difference is that they expect information to come to them, whether it's via the Web, email, cell phone, online chat, whatever. And given the tip of the iceberg of technology we're seeing, it's going to have a big impact on how they expect to receive library services." What this means is that libraries need to start adjusting now. Jenny Levine, the author of The Shifted Librarian, terms this technology adjustment "shifting" and challenges today's libraries "to start meeting these kids' information needs in their world, not [ours]."[4]

Today, more than 25 million children between 2 and 17 years of age in the United States use the Internet routinely, and by 2005 the number is expected to surpass 44 million.[5] Given this fact and the technology-driven world that children are growing up in, it is not surprising to learn that children prefer the Internet over any other medium when it comes to receiving information. An April 2002 study found that in the United States, 33 percent of children between 8 and 17 years of age would choose the Internet over telephone, radio, and even television when allowed to select their preferred information medium.[6] This is a clear shift in preference from the heyday of the TV. Of course, television was a close second for nearly 26 percent of the children, but only when they were restricted to one type of medium. Print resources, such as newspapers and magazines, were included in the survey, but they were rarely identified as a preferred choice. Only 4 percent of the kids surveyed would choose magazines as a resource and fewer than 1 percent would choose newspapers. The results of the survey are summarized in figure 1-1. Clearly, we can be glad that libraries are not in the newspaper business, although many of us do have large periodical collections dedicated to them.

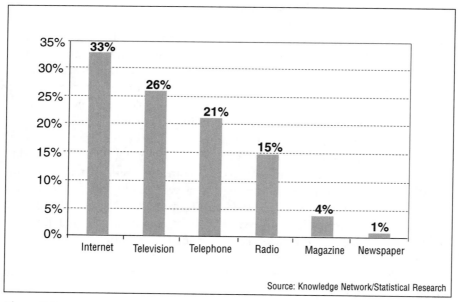

Figure 1-1
What Media Do Children Aged 8 to 17 Years Prefer?

Although books and print media still form the foundation of our libraries, one may well wonder if one day books will entirely disappear. On this front there is good news to report from the child's perspective, as excerpts from an October 2002 web chat with kids reveals.[7] When asked the question "Is the Net better than books?" kids were quick to state their opinions, distinguish differences between the two, and note the benefits of each.

> I think the Net would be awesome if you want to find reference or something, but you can bring a book with you to do some light reading, unlike a computer. Also, it hurts my eyes if I stare at the computer screen too long!!   —Addie, age 13, Illinois

> The net is definitely better! It has everything you can get from a book and loads more! Why bother with books?   —Nick, age 10, Lancaster

> Books are way better than the Net because books don't give you a headache. You also can't read *The Lord of the Rings* on the Internet!
>   —Emma, age 15, Newcastle, UK

> I'm a Net freak and a bookworm! In a book you can disconnect with the real world, get lost in a book, and on the Net you can connect with the whole world. I've met people from all over the world, it's fun!
>   —Eve, age 15, Lincolnshire, UK

Although opinions did vary, the last comment hits the nail on the head and concisely sums up what the majority of kids had to say on the subject. Books allow kids to disconnect from the real world; the Internet allows them to connect with the world. For kids growing up in today's fast-paced environment, each medium has its own advantages.

Another not-so-surprising study was also completed in October 2002 by the NOP Research Group, an internationally recognized research center based in the United Kingdom. That study found that although kids are comfortable with and enjoy books, they actually know more about the Internet.[8] According to the study:

> Six out of ten children knew that a home page was the first page of a website, yet only one in ten (9 percent) could explain what the preface of a book was.

> Fifty-seven percent of kids could identify a hard drive as part of a computer, whereas only one-third of the kids knew that a hardback was a type of book.

Nearly 70 percent of kids knew that "WWW" stood for "World Wide Web," yet fewer than one-quarter knew that "RSVP" was the abbreviation asking them to reply to an invitation.

Although these findings may not be that surprising for many of us in the library profession, they are alarming and should ring a clear wake-up call for all children's libraries. If we are to survive as institutions for children in the future, we need to reinvent ourselves and meet kids' needs in *their world*. With this in mind, chapter 2 explores some examples of libraries that are already on the right track.

NOTES

1. Ohio County Public Library, "Ohio County Public Library Mission Statement," http://wheeling.weirton.lib.wv.us/main/mission.htm (accessed January 19, 2004).
2. Seattle Public Library, "About the Library: Mission Statement," http://www.spl.org/default.asp?pageID=about_mission (accessed January 19, 2004).
3. Public Library of Charlotte and Mecklenburg County, "PLCMC Web Site Mission Statement," http://www.plcmc.org/mission.htm (accessed January 19, 2004).
4. Shifted Librarian, "What Is a Shifted Librarian?" http://www.theshiftedlibrarian.com/stories/2002/01/19/whatIsAShiftedLibrarian.html (accessed January 19, 2004).
5. Grunwald Associates, "Children, Families and the Internet 2000," http://www.grunwald.com/survey/survey_content.html (accessed January 19, 2004).
6. Knowledge Networks, "More Kids Say Internet Is the Medium They Can't Live Without," press release, April 5, 2002, http://www.knowledgenetworks.com/info/press/releases/2002/040502_htm.html (accessed January 19, 2004).
7. CBBC Newsround, "Is the Net Better than Books?" online chat, October 21, 2002, http://news.bbc.co.uk/cbbcnews/hi/chat/your_comments/newsid_2295000/2295723.stm (accessed January 28, 2003; topic now closed).
8. BBC News, "Net Beats Books with Children," October 3, 2002, http://news.bbc.co.uk/2/hi/UK_news/education/2296609.stm (accessed March 10, 2004).

CHAPTER 2

Model Library Websites
for Children

In chapter 1 we highlighted four core areas of children's services: readers' advisory, homework assistance and reference help, programming, and outreach. The Internet offers an opportunity to deliver these services in a new way, allowing children to acquire and interact with information in an environment they find comfortable. Consequently, libraries are discovering ways to offer services online in all four core areas. This can be done in many ways, including transfering traditional informational pathfinders into searchable databases, joining forces with other community organizations in creating original content, and translating existing information into a second language.

Children's libraries have learned there is no point in offering programs or materials that will not appeal to children's interests, and it is important to transfer this concept to any offering created for the Web. Children are more discriminating than adults often give them credit for. They enjoy fun and games, but they can tell the junk from the good stuff. Their attention needs to be captured by things they have not seen somewhere else and by content that will make them want to come back to a website again and again. Bells and whistles are ultimately useless if the accompanying content is not worthwhile. So the challenge in developing engaging sites for children becomes to attract children to the site, offer them a positive online experience, and give them content that makes them want to visit the site again.

This chapter explores library websites that provide core children's services using both new and existing content and that group into familiar categories the services that libraries are known to excel in.

OUTREACH

The practice of taking the library out into the community is older than the traditional library bookmobile. "Outreach" is defined as "the extending of services or assistance beyond current or usual limits."[1] To libraries, outreach can mean finding new ways to reach people who are not traditional library users (such as those who have difficulty getting to the library) and developing ways to better serve patrons by partnering with other community organizations and businesses. Two traditional forms of outreach are storytellers visiting day-care centers and librarians taking materials to nursing homes. But with the advent of the Internet, libraries have gained another important tool that they can use to extend their services beyond their library walls and out into the community.

Traditional Outreach

The traditional approach to library outreach involves physically taking materials and services out in the community. Today, many libraries have expanded on this concept not only by developing innovative services that help patrons navigate and locate information on the Web but also by reaching new patrons that they might not otherwise serve through the Web.

The Las Vegas–Clark County Library District in Las Vegas, Nevada, developed a children's website that puts a new twist on traditional outreach services by combining both a traditional outreach method, a mobile library, with a virtual method. The home page for that site is shown in Figure 2-1. Who could resist a dinosaur wearing shades and typing on a laptop? His name is Neon, and he is the mascot for the Las Vegas–Clark County Library District and the Web on Wheels program. The WOW project offers free programs to elementary-school classes in the Las Vegas area. The programs promote the library with special emphasis on the library's website and electronic resources. The Teachers section allows teachers to sign up online for workshops and gives them tips to help prepare for the visit. The Students Only section is designed to follow up on those workshops. It offers a quiz and an information page about each of the WOW project's nine presentation topics, which include storytelling, science projects, and Webilicious!—a program about how to use online resources. The information pages contain book recommendations, illustrated by cover art, that link to the library catalog and electronic resources. There is also a link to an amazing information guide on the library's main website, a combined resource for children, teens, and adults. The beautiful pathfinders feature recommended books, media (music, videos, etc.), and websites that pertain to a search topic; links to local resources; and a description of several library databases and what specific, topic-related information can be found in each. The guides are clearly organized and offer an activity section with word searches and other learning games, crafts, and a quiz designed to increase a user's knowledge of the subject. WOW is right!

Outreach to Special Populations

Outreach can be achieved within the library walls as well by finding ways to serve users who might speak a different language, by offering adaptive-technology services (such as those for the blind), by providing specialized parenting collections, or by furnishing temporary courtesy services to non-

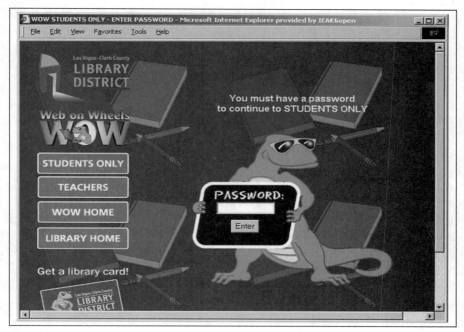

Figure 2-1
WOW Web on Wheels Home Page (http://www.lvccld.org/wow/wow_children.htm), Las Vegas–Clark County Library District, Las Vegas, Nevada

residents. The Internet is a natural conduit for outreach to special patron populations. It lets libraries take relevant information directly to users, often in their own homes, and enables libraries to serve not only local users but a more global community as well. Offering services that users can enjoy from the convenience of home will not keep people away from using the services of the library. Instead, it will increase the value of the library's services to its patrons and allow the library to reach new users who might not otherwise walk through the library's doors.

Web-based materials created just for children are empowering to young minds, and a service that presents information in a non-English-speaking child's primary language can foster a sense of connection that might otherwise be lacking. People whose primary language is not English constitute an increasing percentage of library users. Many public libraries around the country are developing special collections that address the language needs of a growing international population. Spanish language collections have flourished in libraries within the past decade, and numerous libraries are developing collections in other languages that are prominently spoken in their local communities. At many libraries new types of employees, bilingual and cultural specialists, are now offering programming for both children and adults. And on the Web, existing services are being translated into other languages and new projects are being developed to include bilingual capabilities. For example, many libraries have begun to create web directories that offer content and resources in more than one language. The home page for a bilingual story site developed by the Public Library of Charlotte and Mecklenburg County in Charlotte, North Carolina, is reproduced in figure 2-2, and a summer reading page created by Multnomah County Library in Portland, Oregon, is presented in figure 2-3.

StoryPlace (figure 2-2) is a bilingual story site available in both English and Spanish. Original animated stories, written and developed by children's librarians, have themes for preschool and early-elementary-school students. Each theme has an online story, an interactive activity, a print-out craft, and a book list. Spanish stories and activities mirror their English-language counterparts, and contain both text and narration translated by native Spanish speakers. Some of the stories actually act as mini language lessons by including words from both languages. It is easy to change from one language to the other so that children can experience the story in both English and Spanish. Statistical feedback has indicated that StoryPlace is highly used by non-English speakers as a tool to learn the English language, although that was not an original objective of the project.

The colorful summer reading page of the Multnomah County Library is designed for both English- and Spanish-speaking children, as shown in figure 2-3. Information is translated when appropriate, and similar information is substituted when a Spanish translation is unavailable. Some activities, such as coloring pages, need only the directions translated. Recommended links for crafts and other activities that go with the theme (which was "Bugs" in 2002) offer an alternative list of links to Spanish websites. This helpful feature allows Spanish-speaking children to participate in the same types of activities as English-speaking children but uses sites in their language so that they will not encounter information they might be unable to read. Similarly, book lists for recommended reading are not just translated; they contain books written (or translated into) Spanish.

Figure 2-2
StoryPlace Home Page (http://www.storyplace.org), Public Library of Charlotte and Mecklenburg County, Charlotte, North Carolina

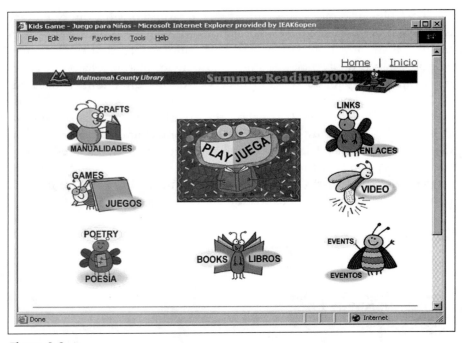

Figure 2-3
Bilingual Summer Reading Page (http://www.multcolib.org/summer/2002/kids/
index.html), Multnomah County Library, Portland, Oregon

Outreach Partnerships

Another way to extend services beyond the library's current limits is by
partnering with other community organizations and businesses. Such partnerships are perfect for grant opportunities or private sector funding, and
the Web is a perfect place to share those partnerships with the world.
Beyond the obvious financial benefits, working with businesses gives libraries
access to specialized knowledge and resources they might not normally have.
There are benefits for businesses that partner with private and community
organizations as well. Businesses that support not-for-profit endeavors are
seen as family-oriented and benevolent to the community, and they enjoy
high visibility and free media coverage when the project is unveiled.

Many community organizations, especially those that work with children, share common goals with public libraries and welcome new ways to

serve their beneficiaries. Collaborative efforts typically lead to resource sharing, enhanced idea development, cross-promotion, and higher-quality results. The result may be a one-time activity, a long-term project, a facility, or a website. If a website is not the end goal, it may certainly be an important by-product of the project. A website can also be used to create awareness of a project before it begins. Community partnerships can support children's issues such as literacy development and education. Focusing on these issues can highlight where library materials may be lacking and how a web-based service might fill this gap. Figures 2-4, 2-5, and 2-6 illustrate some innovative library web projects that were created through library-community partnerships.

An Institute of Museum and Library Services (IMLS) grant project, the Hands on Crafts site, shown in figure 2-4, is part of a project called Weaving a Tale of Craft. The project involved combining library resources

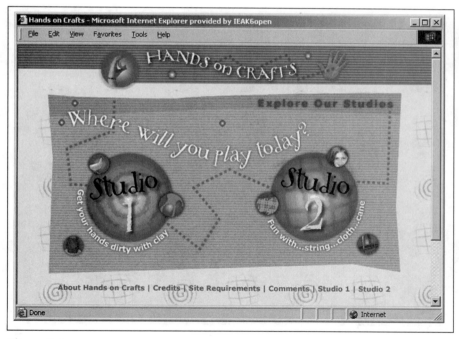

Figure 2-4
Hands on Crafts (http://www.handsoncrafts.org), Public Library of Charlotte and Mecklenburg County and the Mint Museum of Art, Charlotte, North Carolina

with the extensive craft collection of the Mint Museum to create a unique series of workshops, live artist sessions, exhibits, and special events around the foundation of a new informational product, the Hands on Crafts website. The site itself allows children to actively participate in multimedia interactive studios that focus on the fun of doing traditional North Carolina crafts while teaching about the art of pottery, weaving, quilting, and basketry. Videos of their peers and artists at work help children explore the joys of making crafts and creating a masterpiece of their own.

The Satellite Science website, developed by the Phoenix Public Library and the Arizona Science Center, shown in figure 2-5, aims to provide children with a fun way to explore science topics within a library setting." The brightly colored and inviting home page showcases several of the 32 different science topics covered within the site. Each topic has a page that includes descriptions of workshops for local children, activities to try at home, book lists, and recommended science links that anyone can use.

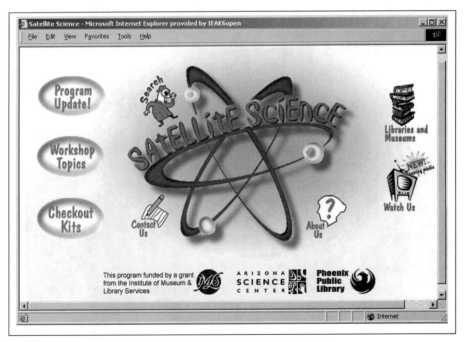

Figure 2-5
Satellite Science (http://www.satellitescience.org), Phoenix Public Library and Arizona Science Center, Phoenix, Arizona

Streaming videos show actual workshops held at libraries and provide an overview of the program. Titles in the book lists link to the children's version of the library's catalog but stay within the Satellite Science site. Some workshops were developed in conjunction with other local agencies, such as the Desert Botanical Garden. Science kits that go with the themes are available for checkout at the library. Satellite Science is a good example of a collaboratively developed website that acts as a centerpiece for a local project and that offers great value for children within the community and for nonlocal users as well.

Wired for Youth (figure 2-6) is a companion site to 10 computer centers funded by the Michael and Susan Dell Foundation and located in branches of the Austin Public Library. Information about the centers themselves, including technology and available workshops, is provided. The majority of the site is a good directory of recommended websites, including

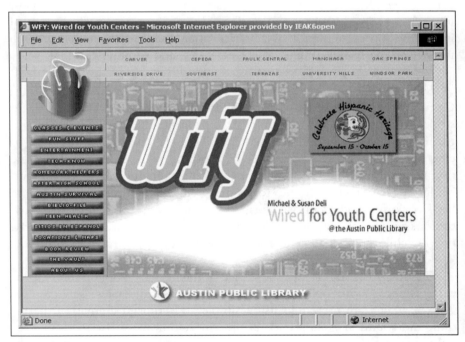

Figure 2-6
Wired for Youth (http://wiredforyouth.com), Austin Public Library and the Michael and Susan Dell Foundation, Austin, Texas

a "tech-know" and a homework help section that describes the library's online resources and includes a list of homework sites in Spanish. Like the computer centers themselves, this site is aimed at both children and young adults. The Wired for Youth site is more than a supplement to the centers; it also serves as an extension of the Austin Public Library's website, which has links to it on both its home page and its youth services page.

Programming

Book talks, craft programs, reading groups, story times, computer classes: there are so many things that children's libraries do well. With so many offerings available, who cares about the Internet? Children do. We know they spend time on the Internet—lots of it—so why not help them to think "library" when they think "Web"? Offering online activities that supplement in-library programs or presenting programs partially or completely online can bring new dimensions to your children's services. Such tie-ins extend the physical space of the library and add a dimension to your library's web presence beyond basic logistical information. Examples of innovative programming that libraries offer children through the Web include online stories, online books, activities, and summer reading.

ONLINE STORIES

One of the most beloved aspects of children's services is story time. Sharing stories with others is a wonderful way to promote the love of reading, and the Internet, with its multimedia capabilities, offers yet another way to engage children in a story-time activity. Nothing will ever replace the magic of a real story time, but online stories offer possibilities for both fun and reading development. Online stories may be electronic versions of favorite books or original content with formats ranging from simple text with illustrations to eye-catching animations with sound. There are several ways to provide children with an online story experience, as illustrated in figures 2-7, 2-8, and 2-9.

Talking Tales (figure 2-7), a service of the Calgary Public Library, provides children with online versions of several classic tales, such as *The Turnip,* which are presented using simple and colorful animation, narration, and sound. This approach brings the traditional dial-a-story into an online environment by adding a visual component. When a story is selected, it is displayed on a virtual book page. Once started, the story plays through automatically so that it can be viewed and experienced without the distraction of page turning. Command buttons directly beneath the story (pause, play, and start again) let a child stop or replay the story. The color-ful animation is presented so simply that it is easy to see why this site would be especially enjoyable for younger children.

StoryPlace (figure 2-8), developed by the Public Library of Charlotte and Mecklenburg County, features original animated stories with online or printable activities and book lists. Preschool stories and interactive activities are completely narrated to assist young readers in developing literacy skills. The elementary stories are partially narrated and allow a child to participate in their creation by selecting or naming certain characters. Choices, action, and visual attractiveness make the site easy to use and enjoyable to watch.

Story Hour (figure 2-9), at the Internet Public Library, is a collection of stories in a variety of formats, from simple text with illustrations to more complicated multimedia presentations that require plug-ins. Children can read and watch an automated slide-show version of *The Fisherman and His Wife* and other tales or page through an unnarrated version of the story with their mouse. Most of the stories give several viewing options, which

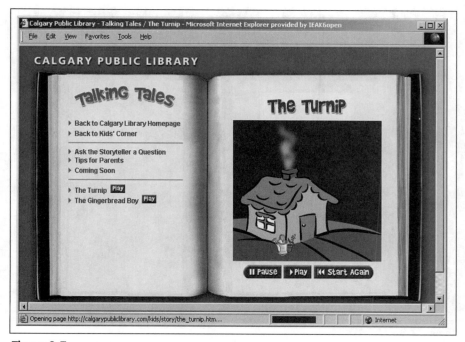

Figure 2-7
Talking Tales (http://calgarypubliclibrary.com/kids/story/welcome.htm), Calgary Public Library, Calgary, Alberta, Canada

allows children with older computers or limited browser capabilities to enjoy the stories in a basic form. All the formats, whether multimedia or not, offer charming illustrations. The stories vary in complexity from nursery rhymes to longer folktales, so this entertaining site is appropriate for preschool to upper-elementary-school children. With its wide mix of formats, the site also demonstrates several imaginative approaches to translating stories for the Web.

ONLINE BOOKS

Another form of children's stories is electronic books, or e-books. Similar to online stories, e-books are usually digital versions of existing print titles but may also be original stories specially developed for this new medium. Some e-books need to be purchased or subscribed to. The benefits of this option include title recognition, good production quality, and the ability to offer books in a different format. Drawbacks include cost, dealing with

Figure 2-8
StoryPlace Preschool Theme (http://www.storyplace.org), Public Library of Charlotte and Mecklenburg County, Charlotte, North Carolina

plug-ins, and inability to control content. Other e-books are available free of charge. Sources such as the International Children's Digital Library (ICDL), TumbleBooks, and Between the Lions enable libraries to provide online books for children without creating the web content themselves.

The International Children's Digital Library

The ICDL(http://icdlbooks.org) is a joint project of the University of Maryland and the Internet Archive, with funding from sources including IMLS and the National Science Foundation. The goal of this project is to build an international collection that reflects both the diversity and the quality of children's literature. Currently, the collection includes materials donated from 27 cultures in 15 languages. Children helped to design the interface that is used to read the books. The collection includes both historical public domain material, such as *Alice in Wonderland,* and contemporary copyrighted material, such as *Axle the Freeway Cat* (donated by

Figure 2-9
Story Hour at the Internet Public Library (http://ipl.sils.umich.edu/div/kidspace/storyhour), School of Information, University of Michigan, Ann Arbor, Michigan

author Thatcher Hurd). The Library of Congress and publishers such as Scholastic donated some of the books. In addition to offering literature to children freely via the Web, the primary function of the collection is to serve as the basis for ongoing research concerning the development and use of digital materials by children and librarians. This site's system requirements, which are fairly high, include a PIII or higher processor, 256 RAM, and the latest version of Java. Adobe Reader is needed for some titles. More details on this project are available on the website.

TumbleBooks

TumbleBooks (http://www.tumblebooks.com) are animated, talking picture books that are online versions of titles from publishers such as Scholastic and Candlewick Press. The stories can be read aloud and paged through manually or played through automatically. As text is being read aloud, it appears highlighted on the screen. Libraries can subscribe to the collection of e-books, which can accommodate unlimited simultaneous use of a collection of titles. Among the titles are *The Paper Bag Princess,* by Robert Munsch, and *Tops and Bottoms,* by Janet Stevens. The collection also includes games and puzzles. Several public libraries offer TumbleBooks to their young patrons, including Richmond Public Library in British Columbia, Canada (http://www.tumblebooks.com/library/asp/home_tumblebooks.asp), and Los Angeles Public Library Kids' Path (http://www.lapl.org/kidspath/coolsites/bookauthor.html#Stories).

Stories at Between the Lions

These stories on the Public Broadcasting System website (http://pbskids.org/lions/stories.html) are designed to be read aloud by parents with their children. Many stories are excerpts of popular children's books. The stories are several pages long, with brief text and an illustration on each page. Clicking on an arrow or the number of the next page advances the story. Words that appear in red are hyperlinked to the Word Helper feature that explains the use of a word and reads the word aloud. A game activity follows each story. Information is provided on how to link to the Between the Lions site.

ACTIVITIES

Another aspect of children's programming in libraries is learning activities that enhance reading programs. Finger plays and songs make story times fun, and special programs give children a chance to explore a variety of interests. In a generation of computer and video games, bringing library activities online is a wonderful enticement to show children how much fun libraries can be. Online activities not only provide supplemental things that children can do at home but also support the programming done within individual library branches. Several approaches can be taken to include activities on a children's website. The most basic is to provide links to existing sites with activities and games. Such activities may be literature-oriented or may reflect what is currently popular with children. Another option is to provide original activities created by the children's librarians or library staff. These may be built from the ground up or based on existing templates (such as freeware Java scripts). Online activities not only "edutain" children but also motivate them to become regular website and library visitors. Figures 2-10, 2-11, and 2-12 present some fine examples of online activities created by libraries.

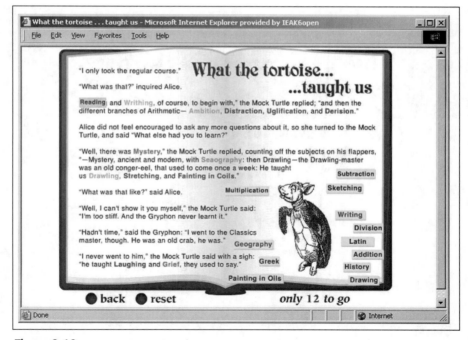

Figure 2-10
Mock Turtle Activity (http://www.princeton.edu/~cotsen/book/mock_turtle.html), Costen Children's Library of Princeton University, Princeton, New Jersey

The Mock Turtle Activity (figure 2-10), part of the Costen Children's Library site, features many resourceful tools for children's librarians, including a fun interactive wordplay activity. The activity's focus is the spoonerisms in the Mock Turtle passage from *Alice in Wonderland,* by Lewis Carroll. The objective is to replace Turtle's muddled words with the words he really meant to say, chosen from a list of understandable words. A counter lets children track how many words are left to solve. Children will unknowingly develop important language skills while caught up in the humor of this game. The simple matching task is greatly enhanced by the click-and-drag capabilities of the Web, an action that most young children are already skilled at.

The Calgary Public Library has developed several online activities for children, including Mystery Hangman, Face Detective, and Battleship. Mystery Hangman and Battleship, which are online versions of familiar games, pit the player against the computer. Face Detective, shown in figure 2-11, is a memory game in which players reconstruct an animated face,

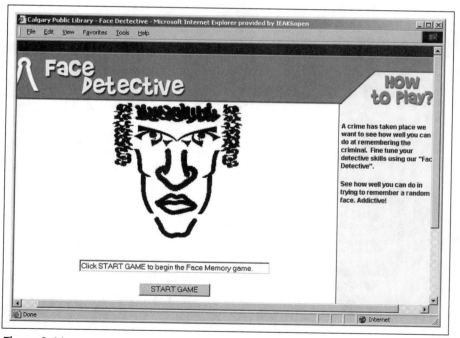

Figure 2-11
Face Detective (http://calgarypubliclibrary.com/kids/games.htm), Calgary Public Library, Calgary, Alberta, Canada

hidden after appearing briefly, by selecting the correct nose, mouth, and so forth. The games were created with JavaScript freeware. One advantage to using activities created in this way rather than links to game sites is that there is no commercial advertising to distract young users. The games are changed periodically to encourage children to visit again and to check out what other cool stuff the library has to offer. Additional games can be found in the Summer Reading area.

The All Fun section of KidsPoint (figure 2-12), a website of the Central Rappahannock Regional Library, has a Quiz Yourself activity that allows children to have some fun while testing their knowledge. Questions in the quizzes are about topics such as Dr. Seuss and the Wright brothers. The quizzes act as an introduction to the topic, challenging children to see how much they already know. The simple quiz structure uses radio buttons that children can click on and offers instant feedback on whether the answer chosen is correct or incorrect. In addition to the quizzes, each topic includes links to activities, games, and further information.

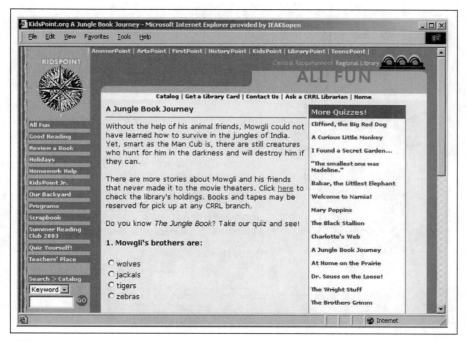

Figure 2-12
KidsPoint (http://www.kidspoint.org/quiz.asp?quiz_id=16), Central Rappahannock Regional Library, Fredericksburg, Virginia

SUMMER READING

Whiling away lazy summer days with a favorite book, keeping track of how much you have read, and celebrating with other readers—these are the joys of summer reading. The Web can be a great supplement to in-library summer reading programs by providing information, book recommendations, online activities, reading records, and ways to communicate with other readers. Some libraries, including our own, are experimenting with online registration and are even putting entire programs online in an effort to take advantage of the tracking and record-keeping tools that can be implemented through the Web. The websites in Figures 2-13 through 2-16 illustrate how several libraries have taken summer reading online.

The State Library of Florida's summer reading program (figure 2-13) offers many examples of original interactive activities developed to supplement traditional programming. Both printout and interactive activities can be found online. Interactive activities include a slider puzzle and a jigsaw

Figure 2-13
FLYP Summer Reading Program Interactive Activity (http://dlis.dos.state.fl.us/bld/flyp2002), Florida Library Youth Program (FLYP), State Library of Florida, Tallahassee, Florida

puzzle, both based on the summer reading artwork. There are a face-drawing activity and a coloring page that children can use to create artwork online. A neat hidden-objects activity lets children point and click on a black-and-white picture to make objects magically display in color when they are found. These activities were created with Java applets, tailored when possible to the summer reading theme. Another intriguing activity is a chat with the program's mascot, Flyp. Children answer questions from Flyp online, such as what is the title of their favorite book. The answers become part of a response from Flyp, and the conversation continues for several pages. The input is simple and the feedback is immediate and personalized, which makes this an excellent example of how a library can use a dynamic activity to reach children in their digital world.

By adding an online reading log and a place to write book reviews (figure 2-14), the Central Rappahannock Regional Library has transformed its site from a mere supplement to a completely redesigned summer reading

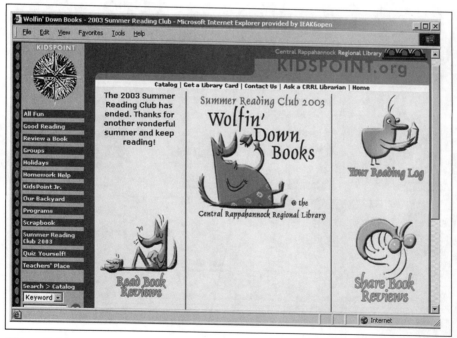

Figure 2-14
KidsPoint Summer Reading Club (http://www.kidspoint.org/src2003), Central Rappahannock Regional Library, Fredericksburg, Virginia

program that fully utilizes the Web. Book recommendations and games are also included. Children create online accounts that enable them to use the reading log and book review features. This personalization not only helps children to build their own special place but also facilitates staff documentation of participation and program effectiveness. The reading log and reviews remain posted after summer reading has ended.

Hennepin County Library's summer reading site includes several interactive games created to enhance and supplement its standard programming. Among our favorites is the Who Had a Bright Idea? matching game (figure 2-15). To play the game, children must drag the appropriate invention to the name of its inventor. If a correct match is made, a picture of the inventor appears. Another favorite, the Lost Animals game, works similarly by matching animal characters to book titles. There are also several jigsaw puzzles based on cover art. A Solve the Mystery activity challenges children

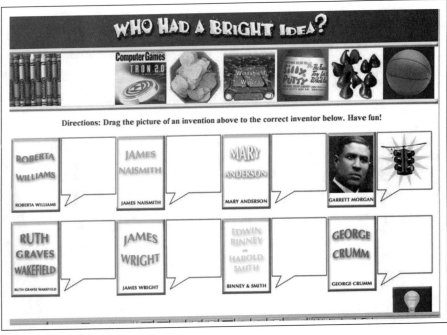

Figure 2-15
Who Had a Bright Idea? Matching Game (http://www.hclib.org/extranet/kid/frame .cfm?frame=/kid/summer/games.cfm), Hennepin County Library, Minnetonka, Minnesota

to type in letters to complete the names of popular mystery characters such as the Hardy Boys. A correct answer results in a comment about the book and a brief appearance of the cover art. Games from previous years are available and their concepts are reused to add familiarity from year to year. By examining several similar games, it is possible to see how one game concept is recycled for each summer's new reading theme. Macromedia Authorware was used to create these activities and does require a plug-in.

The engaging Splish Splash Read! 2002 site (figure 2-16) offers children of all ages lots of fun online activities to supplement the New York Public Library's 2002 summer reading program. Book reviews and reading recommendations are broken into groups by grade level, and children can even submit reviews of their own. Appropriate activities and games are available for all ages, and the site uses polls to gather feedback from users. All in all, this site is colorful and engaging, and offers children (from preschoolers to teens) lots of online fun to increase their participation in summer reading.

Figure 2-16
Splish Splash Read! 2002 (http://summerreading.nypl.org/read2002), New York Public Library, New York, New York

READERS' ADVISORY

Guiding children to great books and fostering a lifelong love of reading can be a daunting task. Librarians traditionally depend on readers' advisory books and expertly generated book lists created in their libraries to keep up with the ever-expanding body of children's literature. The Web allows librarians not only to share this wealth of knowledge with each other but also to create Internet tools that allow children to locate books they can read. Children can use such tools in many ways. Easy-to-use search tools can allow them to search by a favorite author, title, key word, or related books. Some tools may even allow them to post comments and reviews of their own or personalize their own book list—all factors that help grab the interest of a child. Readers' advisory sites geared toward children need to be attractive and engaging for young users, not just a mirror of adult tools with a few illustrations. The option of providing input creates a sense of ownership for each child and is a powerful tool that encourages repeated visits to a site.

Book Lists

Book lists are the core of readers' advisory services for youth libraries. With the advent of the Internet, recommended reading lists can now be accessed by children, parents, and teachers from their homes. Furthermore, reading lists can be linked to reviews, to author pages, and in some cases directly to the library catalog to check availability. By incorporating these enhancements, book lists evolve into true pathfinders, inviting not only the reading of books but also the exploration of ideas. A good starting point for a book list site is the collection of reading lists that the library has already compiled. The web format allows easy access to these lists in the library as well as at home, and many different applications are possible.

STANDARD BOOK LISTS

Standard book lists are lists of books and their authors, usually categorized by subjects or themes. This type of list works particularly well for concept picture books because detailed description is unnecessary. Some examples are shown in figure 2-17 and figure 2-18.

The list in figure 2-17 is found in the On-Lion for Kids! Recommended Reading section of the New York Public Library (NYPL) website. It capitalizes on the well-earned reputation of the NYPL to offer an extra element of authority, and even the title of the book list makes users sit up and pay attention. The titles are not only well chosen but also presented in a way that immediately catches a visitor's notice.

The collection of book lists shown in figure 2-18, which is part of Sign of the Owl, the Chicago Public Library's children's website, contains both annotated and standard lists. Book lists cover four subject lists (adventure, fantasy, science, and funny) grouped by grade level and a preschool list called Look out Kindergarten, Here I Come! An author list, Great Reads for Kids, lists 125 recommended authors and the ages that their books are most appropriate for. Each author's name is hyperlinked to his or her website, if there is one.

ANNOTATED BOOK LISTS

This type of list typically includes brief plot descriptions and author information. By providing brief glimpses of what the stories are about, annotated lists invite children to read the books to discover more. Annotations

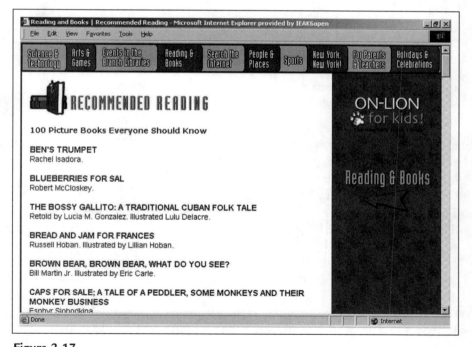

Figure 2-17
100 Picture Books Everyone Should Know (http://www.nypl.org/branch/kids/gloria.html), New York Public Library, New York, New York

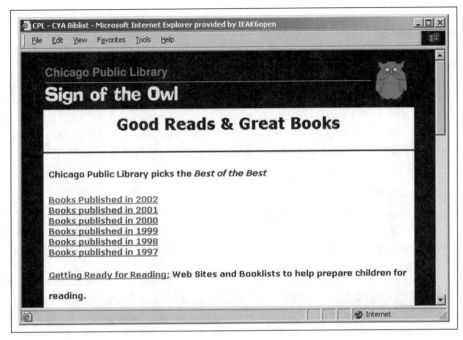

Figure 2-18
Good Reads and Great Books (http://www.chipublib.org/008subject/003cya/
biblist.html), Chicago Public Library, Chicago, Illinois

can also provide information about whether a book is a sequel or features the same characters as related books. Two websites that offer annotated book lists are illustrated in figures 2-19 and 2-20.

The Kids' Webrary (figure 2-19), a portal site of the Morton Grove Public Library, has an excellent compilation of book lists, mostly annotated. The home page of the Book Lists section is a list of lists, with links to a page of annotated titles for each subject. Some topics are traditional favorites, such as fantasy, humor, and historical fiction. Others are more unusual, such as "Differently Abled Kids" and "Buried Treasure: Wonderful Books You Probably Didn't Know About." Annotations are very descriptive, and each title in the list is a hyperlink to the title in the library catalog. One subject does not lead to a book list, yet this is the perfect place for it. The Harry Potter Guide is a two-part list of facts, definitions, character descriptions, and more—an annotated glossary to the world of Harry and his friends. These book lists and extra features are a wonderful example of how readers' advisory services can be presented on the Web.

Figure 2-19
Kids' Webrary Home Page (http://www.webrary.org/kids/jbibmenu.html),
Morton Grove Public Library, Morton Grove, Illinois

The interesting What Do I Read Next? list in figure 2-20 recommends titles that might interest readers who enjoy Living Books and other CD-ROM titles. Each CD-ROM title is annotated and lists the age range of children most likely to be interested in its story and activities. An annotated suggested reading list of two to five book titles accompanies each CD-ROM title. This is a great bridge list that guides children to books based on an established interest.

Reviews

A book review can be described as an extended annotation. It offers the reader more detail and often contains the reviewer's opinion about the book. Reading (or age) level and page numbers may also be provided. On a children's site, the intended audience is an important factor. Even though their subject is the same children's book, a review written for a child should

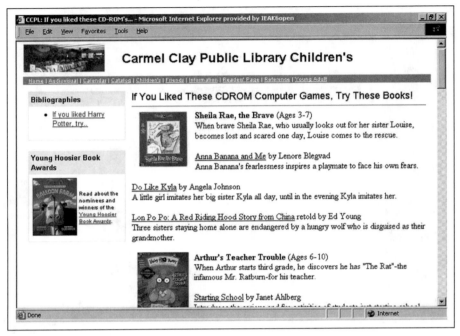

Figure 2-20
If You Liked These CD-ROMs . . . (http://www.carmel.lib.in.us/child/cdroms.htm),
Carmel Clay Public Library, Carmel, Indiana

differ significantly from a review written for an adult. Whether written by
adults or children, children's book reviews can either stand on their own or
be the focal point of an online reading center.

REVIEWS BY ADULTS

Reviews written by adults for children should have child-friendly language
and presentation, and should be designed to help children choose books that
would appeal to them. Three library sites that include book recommendations written by adults for children are shown in figures 2-21 through 2-23.

BookHive (figure 2-21), a site from the Public Library of Charlotte
and Mecklenburg County, combines staff reviews of books with children's
comments about them. The reviews may be searched by title or author or
browsed by category, and results may be further limited to a general reading level (preschool, primary, intermediate, and so forth). In addition, children can create book lists of favorite titles with personal comments about

them, retrieve the information later, and even e-mail it to friends. This site easily contains over a thousand staff reviews. Additional content supports the book reviews, including Zinger Tales—videos of storytellers such as Jackie Torrence sharing their craft. A Harry Potter quiz, printable coloring pages, and bookplates round out this rich children's reading site.

The Burlington Public Library children's staff writes most of the child-friendly reviews for Cool Reads (figure 2-22), with a few reviews submitted by adult library volunteers. A new set of reviews is posted for each season, and previous sets are archived for easy access. The reviews, which use icons to identify subject categories and stars for ratings, are accompanied by a clear key posted at the top of the page. The reviews are grouped into early chapter books and fiction, with the reviews of easier titles appropriately shorter than reviews for the fiction titles. These reviews would be useful and interesting to both adults and children. Monthly staff favorites are listed, and there are links to reviews of books nominated for Canadian children's book awards.

Figure 2-21
BookHive Book Review Search (http://www.bookhive.org), Public Library of Charlotte and Mecklenburg County, Charlotte, North Carolina

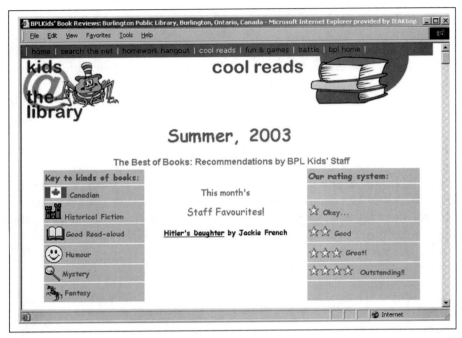

Figure 2-22
Cool Reads (http://www.bpl.on.ca/kids/reviews.htm), Burlington Public Library,
Burlington, Ontario, Canada

In Staff Book Picks for Kids (figure 2-23), developed by the Waukesha
Public Library, reviews by two staff librarians offer plot summaries and
explain why children might enjoy each story. The page is clearly organized.
Each review denotes whether a book is a picture book or juvenile fiction
and is accompanied by cover art. These reviews are a nice addition to the
book list section of this children's website.

REVIEWS BY CHILDREN

Reviews written by children for children examine a book from a child's-eye
view, which might be analytical, descriptive, opinionated (positive or negative), or a combination of all three. Child-written reviews not only offer
information to fellow readers but also provide opportunities for self-expres-
sion. The encouragement of this type of creative input can be very empowering for children and also rewarding to staff.

Figure 2-23
Staff Book Picks for Kids (http://www.waukesha.lib.wi.us/kc/staffpicks.shtml),
Waukesha Public Library, Waukesha, Wisconsin

Several public libraries have expanded the concept of including book reviews for children on their websites by allowing children themselves to write the reviews. Reviews can be gathered manually, but collecting them via the website extends opportunities for participation to a much larger user base. Examples of library applications for reviews written by children for children are presented in figures 2-24 and 2-25.

The Review Crew section of Louisville Free Public Library's Kids Pages provides children with access to reviews written by their peers (figure 2-24). Children can use a simple form to submit book reviews and story ideas of their own. Reviews from past years are archived and available. The site is clean, attractive and very user friendly.

On the Carmel Clay Public Library website (figure 2-25), children write reviews based on questions about their reading experiences with a book. The review displays the questions along with the child's answers.

Books are categorized by reading level and may also be searched by title and author. The child's first name and age and the date that the review was submitted are included with each review.

ANIMATED REVIEWS

Animated reviews are definitely a new twist on readers' advisory and provide a novel approach to delivering books reviews for children. The Danbury Public Library is one of the first libraries we have found to explore this new option. Using a subscription-based service (http://www.readthe books.com), the site provides children with book reviews that are told by animated characters. The animations are amusing, although in some reviews it is difficult to find the relationship between the narrator and the story. To view this new, innovative application, visit the Danbury Public Library Read the Book page at http://www.readthebooks.com/rtb/files/ rtb_danbury/aliens/general/composeGeneral.mv.

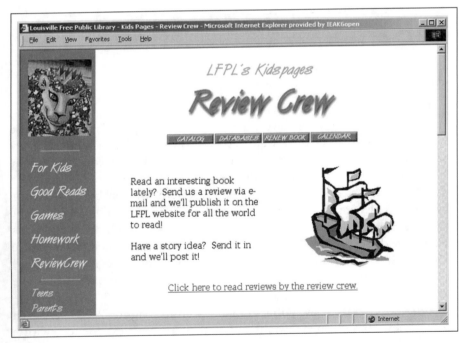

Figure 2-24
Review Crew (http://www.lfpl.org/kidspages/POPCHBKS.HTM), Louisville Free Public Library, Louisville, Kentucky

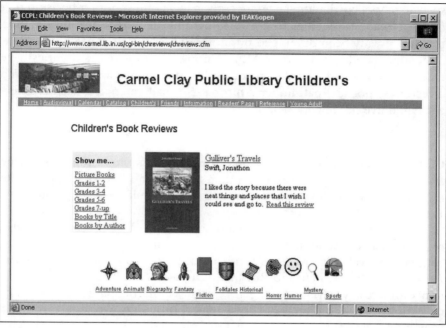

Figure 2-25
Children's Book Reviews (http://www.carmel.lib.in.us/cgi-bin/
chreviews/chreviews.cfm), Carmel Clay Public Library, Carmel, Indiana

HOMEWORK ASSISTANCE

One area that lends itself well to the online environment is homework assistance. Students often think of the Internet first when they need to find information, and children are starting to surf the Web at increasingly younger and younger ages. Lack of discretionary searching can lead students to inaccurate or inappropriate information or may simply leave them confused or overwhelmed. A library can offer a valuable service by guiding students to quality, authoritative information on the Internet and teaching them how to differentiate between online resources, such as encyclopedias and databases, and Internet sites.

The first decision that must be made when considering an Internet homework assistance tool is what type of homework assistance to offer. Categorized collections of websites, bibliographic instruction, subscription resources, and interactive live assistance are some options that can be offered individually or in conjunction with each other. Services that tie into specific school curriculum areas are especially helpful. Another decision that must be made is whether to create something new or to use information that has already been developed by another library or organization, such as a recommended site list from ALA. Among the approaches libraries have taken in tackling the challenge of online homework assistance are web directories, portals, pathfinders, tutorials, e-mail reference, virtual reference, and live homework help.

Web Directories

Gathering websites that offer good information on school topics is a large task, and organizing the results so that students can find sites appropriate for their needs is an even larger one. The result is a web directory. Yahooligans! defines a web directory as "a collection of websites put into an order that's easy to browse through or search."[2] Web directories are also referred to as subject guides. Yahoo! and Yahooligans! are examples of large commercial web directories. *Delivering Web Reference Services to Young People*, by Walter Minkle and Roxanne Hsu Gledman, further categorizes a noncommercially developed directory as a "young people's web reference collection."[3] A web directory allows logical browsing, working through a topic from general to specific, as in a self-directed reference interview. This process eliminates the keyword and typing challenges of searching. Many web directories are also searchable, but they differ from search engines in that they search only the sites found within the directory, not the entire Web. Each suggested site in a homework assistance directory should be annotated with a clear description that will help students decide whether to investigate what that site has to offer. Figures 2-26 through 2-28 show examples of student homework directories created by libraries.

Multnomah County Library offers an amazingly thorough directory of websites that is arranged to make it easy to find common homework topics (figure 2-26). There are 39 general homework topics listed on the main page. Each general topic links to a page of related subtopics. The science topic on the main page, for example, links to a page that lists 29 science topics (such as chemistry and biomes), several of which are broken down even further to help students get to specific information. Separate pages are used when necessary to help reduce scrolling. Hyperlinks make the browsing setup very navigable and easy to follow, and the annotations are clearly written. The Multnomah County School Corps Department works closely with local schools to match resources with curriculum and thus ensure that the library's web directory will be highly relevant and useful for students everywhere.

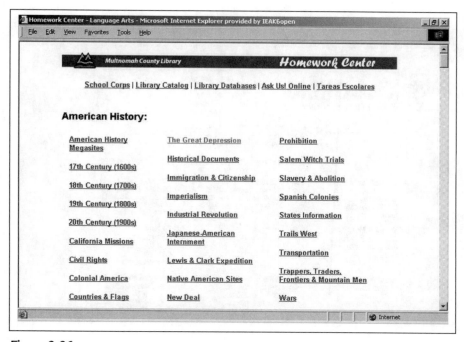

Figure 2-26
Homework Center: American History Web Directory (http://www.multcolib.org/homework/index.html), Multnomah County Library, Portland, Oregon

The searchable KidsClick! directory (figure 2-27) was developed with a Library Services and Technology Act (LSTA) grant by the Ramapo County Library System and is currently maintained by the Colorado State Library. Thousands of sites are organized into over 600 subjects that can be browsed, searched alphabetically, or searched by keyword. The subjects can also be viewed by Dewey numbers if preferred. Simple and advanced searches are available. There are links to search tools appropriate for children to assist with basic, image, and sound searches. Each site listed has a clear description of its content, level of illustration (none, some, or many), reading level by grade range, and subject. A link is provided back to the main subject list, which is helpful for finding similar sites when a user starts with a general keyword search. Search lessons are also included (see Tutorials). KidsClick! contains an impressive collection of subjects and sites with flexible search and browsing options, and shows that the Web does indeed have great content for kids and that it is possible to guide kids to that content.

Figure 2-27

KidsClick! Web Search (http://www.kidsclick.org), Ramapo Catskill Library System, Middletown, New York

Similar to Morton Grove's well-known adult Webrary, the Kids' Webrary is a searchable collection of links grouped by general Dewey decimal classifications (figure 2-28). Since each number range has a description (for example, 100–199: Problems, Feelings, and Behavior), the collection acts as a learning tool to develop search skills that can be used in the physical library and in the online catalog. Individual sites and other directory sites are included, each with a description.

Portals

A good definition for a portal is "systems which gather a variety of useful information resources into a single, 'one stop' web page, helping the user to avoid being overwhelmed . . . or feeling lost on the Web."[4] In other words, a portal provides a method of reorganizing and presenting information to make it easier for an individual to use. A portal differs from a web

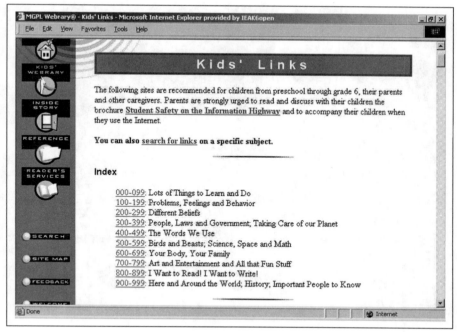

Figure 2-28
Kids' Webrary Links (http://www.webrary.org/kids/jkidslinks.html), Morton Grove
Library, Morton Grove, Illinois

directory in that it offers some level of customization. A student may customize a portal by selecting or adding favorite resources. Libraries may customize a portal created for use by many libraries by tailoring it to the needs of their specific communities.

Some portals deal only with links to websites, while others may allow individualized access to subscription resources or other personalization tools, such as local weather or an events calendar. Levels of customization may also vary, from the addition of a library logo to the choice of how a page looks. Two examples of portals for students are presented in figures 2-29 and 2-30.

The Start Squad Kids' Portal (figure 2-29) is part of a statewide North Carolina initiative called "The Very Best Place to Start," an awareness campaign "to elevate libraries to 'top of mind' for parents, caregivers, and others who want to connect children and teens with learning and discovery." Jim Rosinia, Youth Services Consultant with the State Library of North Carolina, explains how the idea of including a youth portal as part of this campaign originated: "Early in the process, State Library staff working on

Figure 2-29
Start Squad Kids' Portal (http://startsquad.org), State Library of North Carolina, Raleigh, North Carolina

the campaign heard a recurring message from youth services librarians: they wanted to be able to do more with kids that involved the Web but they lacked the time (and some felt that they lacked the technical expertise) to locate quality sites and develop web pages with links to these sites." [5]

The result is Start Squad ("Start" being the tie-in to the overall campaign), a searchable collection of websites organized by category as well as by age group (preschool, elementary, middle school) in a colorful interface featuring Internet guides Lee the Librarian and friends. Start Squad is easily navigable and clearly organized. The search feature upgrades the functionality of a web directory and provides a search alternative to topic browsing. Librarians can customize the site for their users by displaying their library's logo, selecting default sites, limiting topics, and choosing whether students can search the Internet using Google SafeSearch. Although the collection is mostly websites, a few databases from the statewide NC Live collection are included and require authentication. Students using Start

Squad cannot customize it, but they can grade the sites and offer comments. Start Squad is a good example of an interface that was designed for students in both functionality and appeal and that can be shared by and customized for multiple libraries.

The Brarydog portal (figure 2-30) was created by the Public Library of Charlotte and Mecklenburg County mainly for local users, but its features make it appropriate for students anywhere to use. The emphasis is on customization, guided by a friendly blue prairie dog, resulting in a personal "homework help and web companion." To use Brarydog, students create their own personalized page. Students select a user name and password, a greeting name that displays on the page, the colors of the page, and a search tool. They also decide which of the available resources will display on their page. For local users, the option of including their library card number provides access to premium resources (such as library subscription

Figure 2-30
Brarydog Portal (http://www.brarydog.net), Public Library of Charlotte and Mecklenburg County, Charlotte, North Carolina

databases) and provides seamless access to multiple resources without individual library card authentication. Nonlocal users can access the nonpremium resources, which include maps and flags of the world, a North Carolina pathfinder, and several online newspapers. They can also take advantage of a feature that allows them to add up to 25 favorite websites to their personalized page. All users have access to the Brarydog Research Center, which has information on citing resources and how to organize a project, and can do dictionary and thesaurus searches directly from their page. Brarydog is a one-stop shopping mall for homework assistance, customized for each student's individual needs and tastes.

Pathfinders

When a student needs to locate detailed resources on a specific subject, an annotated pathfinder, or webliography, can be of great help. For the sake of this discussion we define a pathfinder as an online annotated bibliography. One could argue that a web directory (a collection of links grouped by subject) is also a pathfinder. But unlike most web directories, pathfinders may include print and other media as well as resources that are available online. Figures 2-31 and 2-32 present examples of student pathfinders that libraries have created.

Potamus Place (figure 2-31), created by the Cleveland Heights–University Heights Public Library, is actually a directory of pathfinders on familiar school research-related topics. For each subject the pathfinder lists websites with descriptions (and sometimes screen shots), books (fiction and nonfiction), videos and CDs, and instructions on how to search for the topic in the online catalog. The listings for library materials display cover art (if available) and provide bibliographic information and even links to the catalog to check availability. This very useful tool is presented in an interesting way.

The School Assignment Database created by the Geauga County Public Library (figure 2-32) is another example of a directory of pathfinders but with an emphasis on school assignments. Each pathfinder is developed to assist with a specific assignment from a teacher. Pathfinders can be found by school or teacher name. The pathfinder begins with the dates and a detailed description of the assignment and any materials restrictions, all of which are provided by the teacher. The rest of the page is the actual pathfinder, with suggested subject headings and Dewey numbers, reference materials found in the library, and online databases and websites. Search

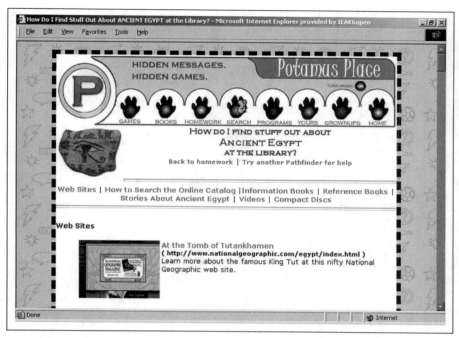

Figure 2-31
Potamus Place Pathfinder (http://www.potamusplace.net/pathfinder.shtml),
Cleveland Heights–University Heights Public Library, Cleveland Heights, Ohio

hints for the databases are provided when needed. The websites are not annotated, but they are specific enough to the topic that descriptions are not necessary. The creation of this helpful tool began with the soliciting of assignments from local teachers in the spring of 2001, and the pathfinders were up and running for the beginning of the school year the following fall. The pathfinders are created by the head of youth services at the teacher's local library branch and written as HTML and posted on the website by the webmaster.[6]

Tutorials

As information becomes more readily available online, the library's role as a trainer in research techniques becomes more vital. Bibliographic instruction can be a time-consuming and difficult task because each person learns in an individual way and at an individual pace. Given that students often go

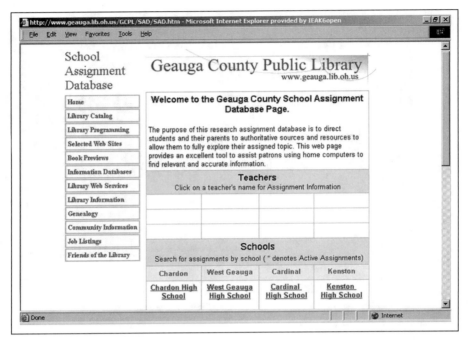

Figure 2-32
Geauga County School Assignment Database (http://www.geauga.lib.oh.us/GCPL/
SAD/SAD.htm), Geauga County Public Library, Chardon, Ohio

online to seek information, one solution is to offer students online instruction on how to find what they need. Online tutorials are not a new concept, but far fewer are available for young people than for adults. Keeping the information interesting while presenting it in an understandable manner is a challenge, especially since the topics, such as search terms and Boolean and research strategies, are overwhelming to begin with. Two approaches currently available online are illustrated in figures 2-33 and 2-34.

Figure 2-33 presents an example of an online tutorial created by the Vancouver Public Library that students can work through at their own pace. Designed for seventh-grade students, the tutorial covers such basics as searching the library and the Web and includes four specific skills modules: Catalogue, Ebsco Resources, eLibray Plus, and the Internet. After completing the introductory module, students select one of four homework areas (Early Man, Plants, Ancient Egypt, or Earth Science—Volcanoes) to use in completing the skills modules. Each module offers

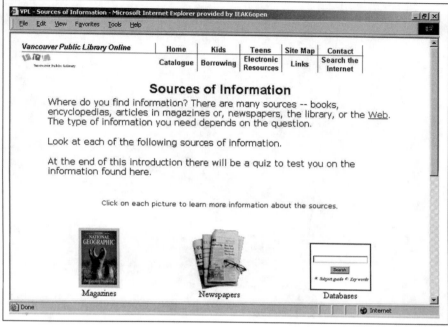

Figure 2-33
Student Tutorial—Sources of Information (http://www.vpl.vancouver.bc.ca/Courses/sources.htm), Vancouver Public Library, Vancouver, British Columbia, Canada

step-by-step instructions on how to use a specific resource. A frame on the left side of the screen displays instructions while the right side of the screen shows the actual resource page. The instructions walk the users through what to do on the resource page, such as where to click and what search terms to enter. When instructions are complete, students move on to the next step of instructions and its accompanying resource page. This is an excellent interactive tutorial showing library-specific resources and using realistic search examples.

The KidsClick! Worlds of Web Searching tutorial (figure 2-34) offers lessons to go along with its directory of websites (figure 2-27). Students begin on the Worlds of Web Searching page, where each planet represents a type of Internet searching. Clicking on a planet selects a lesson. Each lesson uses text and images to provide an overview of a search strategy. Written in child-friendly language, the tutorials are easy to follow. Students just read through a page and click on the arrow at the bottom to continue.

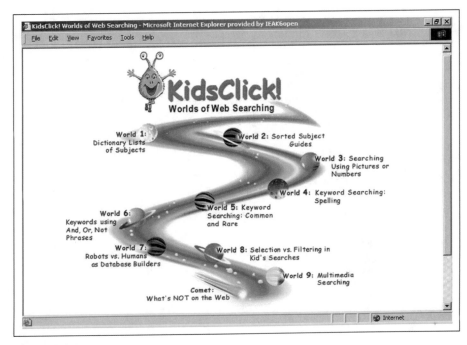

Figure 2-34
KidsClick! Worlds of Web Searching (http://www.rcls.org/wows/index.html),
Ramapo Catskill Library System, Middletown, New York

Although the tutorials are not interactive, there is an activity at the end of each lesson that enables users to practice the skills learned. The lessons are presented simply and cover their topics well. This site shows how basic HTML can be used effectively to create tutorials.

E-mail Reference

Nothing can top interaction with a real person and knowing that someone took the time to personally assist you with your unique question. Although children are inundated with and accustomed to digitization, like adults, they still require assistance and communication with real people—hence the popularity of chat rooms among youth. E-mail reference and live reference offer two options for communicating digitally with students. With e-mail the feedback is not immediate, but it is still personal. Brarydog, a home-

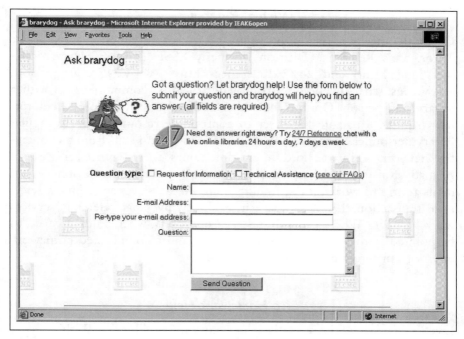

Figure 2-35
Ask Brarydog (http://www.brarydog.net), Public Library of Charlotte and
Mecklenburg County, Charlotte, North Carolina

work portal site for middle and high school students, illustrated in figure 2-35, offers an example of an e-mail reference service for children.

Ask Brarydog, Brarydog's e-mail reference service, employs an online form to collect information from a user (figure 2-35) and sends the answer to the user's e-mail address. The amount of information collected varies. Because the form replaces the traditional reference interview, it was designed to obtain and process as much information as possible. For example, the user's log-in automatically determines whether the user has access to online databases, noted by a library card number in the user's profile, or only to websites This information is forwarded with the student's question to the reference librarian who will respond to the request so that the librarian will know what resources the student has access to. Ask Brarydog also forwards the inquiry to the library's Web Services Department if the request is for technical assistance rather than for reference information.

Virtual Reference

Currently the two largest providers of live-chat reference services are Tutor.com's Reference Division (formerly LSSI) (http://www.vrtoolkit .net/index.html) and 24/7 Reference (http://www.247ref.org). Both services use chat technology to provide real-time communication with a library staff person. Options include co-browsing, which allows the librarian to guide a patron's browser to appropriate resources. Using regular library personnel during standard business hours and staff from a cooperative network of libraries in different time zones, the reference services can be made available 24 hours a day, seven days a week. This is a boon for students trying to work on last-minute homework assignments. Like a reference transaction that takes place in a library, live-chat reference services work best for "Where can I find . . . ?" questions, when students need to be pointed in the right direction. However, more complicated homework questions may require a different approach.

Live Homework Help

Live homework help is a relatively new concept for libraries. Within recent years, several libraries across the country have expanded their homework assistance programs to include Tutor.com's Live Home Help. This subscription service offers students an opportunity to work with a tutor in an electronic classroom using chat-type technology and a shared work space. The student uses the product to select a subject area and a grade level, and then is connected with a tutor in an electronic classroom. Using the whiteboard area of the virtual environment, the student and tutor are able to communicate with each other to work through the student's problem. The library (through its subscription) determines the times the service will be available, and assistance is provided in Spanish as well. Sessions last an average of 15 to 20 minutes. Users report a high level of satisfaction with this service. As one student put it in her closing evaluation: "Wow, this service is great. I now feel better prepared to take my test tomorrow." An example of a Tutor.com virtual math classroom is presented in figure 2-36.

In this chapter we have examined some models of innovative Internet services that libraries have already created in the areas of readers' advisory, homework assistance and reference help, programming, and outreach services. We hope these ideas, from simple to flashy, inspire you to explore how you can develop and offer such services for your young patrons. Now that

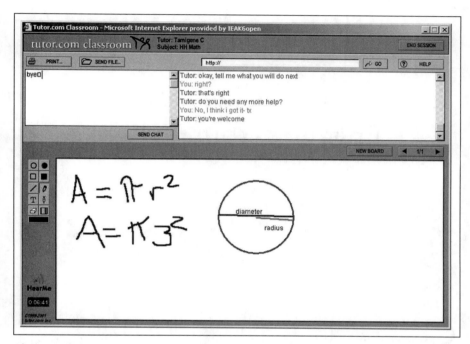

Figure 2-36
Tutor.com Virtual Math Classroom

we have seen what can be done, let's look at the decisions and processes you can use to develop a great children's website of your own.

NOTES

1. *Merriam-Webster OnLine,* http://www.m-w.com (accessed January 19, 2004).
2. Yahooligans! glossary, http://www.yahooligans.com/docs/info/glossary3 .html#web%20directory (accessed April 7, 2003).
3. Walter Minkle and Roxanne Hsu Gledman, *Delivering Web Reference Services to Young People* (Chicago: ALA Editions, 1999), 10.
4. Ibid., 48.
5. Jim Rosinia, e-mail message to author, February 26, 2003.
6. Rachel Hartman, e-mail message to author, April 2, 2003.

CHAPTER 3

Guidelines for
Engaging Young Users

Child and adults not only think and learn differently but also use the Internet differently. As children's librarians who have observed children using computers, we can surely attest to this. How many times have you observed a child enthusiastically engaged in an Internet site full of colorful images and pictures rather than just simple words or text? Such image-heavy websites can drive adults crazy. We want to be able to navigate a website quickly and find what we need, not spend time exploring. Young users find sound and animation especially appealing, even if they serve no real purpose other than to entertain. However, the same features can easily irritate adults because they hinder a site's download time and thwart our ability to locate to what we need. The truth of the matter is that children and adults desire different things from their online interactions. Children tend to be more interested in the online experience and what websites allow them to do, see, or come into contact with. Adults, in contrast, tend to rely on the Internet as more of an information-gathering tool, a way to retrieve and share information rather than an environment for engaging in new experiences. Because the majority of child-oriented websites are designed and created by adults, it is important for us to keep those differing desires in mind as well as some of the other basic differences that separate child and adult Internet users.

A 2002 study conducted by web-usability guru Jakob Nielsen summarizes some of the more prominent differences between children and adults as they relate to Internet usage patterns.[1]

Children strongly desire design elements such as animation and sound because such elements engage many senses. They help to create a strong first impression for children and encourage them to stay and explore. The same design elements often create a negative impression on adults, especially if they appear to offer nothing more than entertainment value.

Children are drawn to large graphical environments and enjoy "Easter-egg-hunting" activities that encourage them to move their mouse around the screen to locate hidden elements. Although adults may initially find this type of design appealing, they quickly tire of it and prefer having information presented to them directly rather than being forced to seek it out.

Children rarely scroll down a web page, preferring to interact with only the information that is visible on the opening screen. Although such behavior was also common among adults in early Internet-user studies, it has disappeared as adults have become savvier users of web browsers and their navigation elements.

Children enjoy graphic metaphoric images (such as pictures of rooms or 3-D maps) that serve as entry points to the various features of a website. Adult users tend to prefer linear or well-laid-out navigation schemes that allow them to view at a glance the structure and content of an entire site.

And surprisingly, children tend to be more willing than adults to actually read instructions on a web page, such as the rules for playing a game. In contrast, most adults hate to read long paragraphs or instructions, preferring instead to dive right into an online activity without first finding out what it's all about.

Many of these distinctions can be attributed to the differences between the types of Internet activities that adults and children frequently engage in. Most young children use the Web primarily for entertainment, to play a game or to engage in a learning activity. As children become older, their online use expands to also encompass homework assignments, surfing, and communication with friends. Because such activities and behaviors are more prominent among younger Internet users, they encourage the use of multimedia design elements (video, graphics, and sound) that allow the child to be both visually and verbally stimulated. For adult users, who often access the Internet in business or professional settings, the use of multimedia design elements can often be inappropriate to the situation and irritating. With those basic differences in mind, we will explore some of the general guidelines that are important to keep in mind when developing online library services for children.

DESIGNING FOR KIDS

Unlike business and informational websites, which are designed primarily for adult users, websites for kids must take everyone into account: children, parents, teachers, grandparents, caregivers, and more. Anyone who is interested in the well-being or education of youth becomes a member of your audience when you design a site targeted to children. Furthermore, the younger the children you are trying to reach, the larger the audience of adult users you will also have to please. To develop a site for so many interested parties may seem like a heavy responsibility to bear—and at times it can be. However, the key to overcoming that challenge is to target your site to your primary audience, children, and to worry only about developing the site for them. If you keep that goal in mind and focus on creating the best possible site for your primary audience, you will succeed in pleasing the majority of your secondary audiences (parents, educators, caregivers, and others) as well.

That guideline, although easy to state, is not always easy to adhere to. The simple fact that we are adults predisposes us to develop websites that are more likely to give priority to our needs and interests as children's specialists rather than to address the needs and interests of children. Unfortunately, it is not too hard to find a children's Internet site (public library, educational, or other—perhaps even your own) that is intended for kids to use but is poorly designed for them. These websites rarely offer screen elements that engage children and encourage them to explore. They tend to be linear in layout as well as content and require children to scroll down through multiple screens to find something of interest. For the most part these pages tend to consist only of links to other children's sites. They are not designed for children (the primary audience) but rather for adults (the secondary audience) to use as tools in locating sites that they can recommend to kids. Granted, these types of Internet pathfinders can be of great value, but if you truly want to reach children, you need to design a site that puts children first.

When developing a website for children, it is also important to narrow down the age range of your audience as much as possible. It is practically impossible to design a one-size-fits-all site for children because children of different ages vary greatly in their needs, interests, and stages of development. Just as your library may group its children's book collection according to reading and comprehension levels (easy reader, chapter books, and so forth), you need to adapt your Internet services to children's specific development stages and Internet preferences as well.

A common method of grouping children that can be adapted for use in developing websites is by level of reading skill: pre-readers, beginning readers, intermediate readers, and young adults.

Pre-readers (3- to 5-Year-Olds)

Preschoolers are full of curiosity, and their language skills are burgeoning. Their fine motor skills are sharpening, and they enjoy using manipulative objects (blocks, puzzles, games) that allow them to sharpen both their physical and their mental skills.[2] Their skills as emergent readers are just beginning to develop, and most of their interaction with books comes from adults reading to them. They recognize letters and perhaps a few small words and begin to pay closer attention to sounds and letters.[3] Their attention spans, as we know well, are very short.

Websites designed primarily for preschoolers depend heavily on engaging and metaphoric graphics that are familiar to youngsters. Activities should be of short duration and use generous amounts of sound and motion to provide feedback. If a site contains reading activities, audio should be included so that users can hear the words as they follow them on the screen. Activities should also allow for repetition. Preschoolers enjoy doing the same things over and over, and feel a huge sense of accomplishment when they master something new.

Beginning Readers (5- to 8-Year-Olds)

Children in the early years of elementary school begin to form their own identities as they become aware that the world extends beyond their immediate surroundings. They can read books with several lines of print and tend to prefer picture books to beginning chapter books, which reinforce their reading skills and comprehension with visual images.

Websites designed primarily for this age range also depend heavily on graphic images that invite youngsters to explore. Since fine reading skills are just beginning to develop, text should be kept to a minimum so that it does not overwhelm the child. When text is displayed on the screen, it should appear in an easily readable font that is large enough for beginning readers. Because this age group's attention span is growing, activities can be longer and allow users to interact with images or text on an individual, self-paced basis.

Intermediate Readers (9- to 12-Year-Olds)

Children in this age group are refining their reading skills and can easily conquer chapter books and juvenile fiction. They begin to think in abstract terms and enjoy participating in activities that involve interactions with their peers.[4] It is at this age that many children begin to use the computer for the first time to interact with their friends through e-mail, bulletin boards, instant messaging, and chat.

Websites designed for this age group start to rely more heavily on text but still focus on visual appeal. Most activities feature single-user interaction and feedback from the computer rather than group-related pursuits. However, this is starting to change as more and more preteen websites are beginning to include speak-your-mind activities such as surveys and polls.

Young Adults (13- to 17-Year-Olds)

Young adults may still be categorized as children, but we all know that they do not want us to think of them as such. Teens definitely want to exercise their independence and explore all options available to them. Teens rule when it comes to using the Internet as a communication tool and are especially fond of instant messaging. A 2001 study found that 74 percent of online teens regularly use instant messaging to communicate with friends, compared to 44 percent of the adult online population.[5] This huge change in how teens interact has occurred in just the past few years and signals the kinds of trends we are likely to see more of.

Such trends must be reflected in well-designed websites for young adults. Good sites for this age group are often developed under the guidance of teen advisory boards or by teens themselves. Those sites speak to the issues affecting teens today and encourage users to return by frequently changing their appearance, design, and content to keep up with current trends.

Designing sites for teenagers carries its own complex set of guidelines and considerations that could easily fill the pages of an entire book. Although we cannot explore all the issues here, it is important for librarians to understand the characteristics of teen Internet users and understand how they compare to the characteristics of other groups of children.

CONTENT GUIDELINES

Start out Simple

When developing a library site for children, it is important to start simple and build gradually toward a larger mission or goal. Do not try to develop too much for kids at once. Begin with a simple objective and focus on doing it well. Young users, like adults, will be more likely to return to your site if you first give them *quality* rather than *quantity*. It is better initially to offer fewer features that are high in quality and easy to use than to offer many features that are mediocre in design or poor in functionality. Negative experiences, for the most part, will discourage children from returning to your site, even if you clearly state that the site is under construction or that more content is being added. Children are highly motivated by positive experiences. Therefore it is better to concentrate on a smaller objective that can be executed well. Once you have achieved that objective, you can begin to expand on it.

An example of a website that started modestly is the BookHive site (figure 3-1) that was created by the Public Library of Charlotte and Mecklenburg County. When the BookHive site was first launched, the staff's simple objective was to provide approximately two dozen new children's book reviews (written to appeal to kids, not for adults) each month in several common genres. As the site grew and attracted more users, the staff decided to add a search component along with an option for kids to contribute their own comments about books. Eventually, after many years, a personalized book list feature was added as well other enhancements that assist children in using the site. The slow and steady growth of the site was based on a series of small goals that systematically led to achieving the long-term goal of providing a comprehensive online guide for children to use in locating quality literature and books. The team of staff members who manage the development and maintenance of the site still adhere to the original—and unchanged—goal of adding 24 new reviews to the database each month. Today, the website's database has grown to over 1,000 reviews and is accessed by more than 40,000 users around the world each month. Its success could not have happened if the staff had not adhered to the "start out simple" rule.

Figure 3-1
BookHive Home Page (http://www.bookhive.org), Public Library of Charlotte and Mecklenburg County, Charlotte, North Carolina

Keeping it simple also applies to the use of good basic design principles. When websites are simply designed to ensure ease of use by adults, they are also likely to be easy to use for kids. Children not only use sites designed for kids but also sites such as Yahoo and the Weather Channel that are designed primarily for adults. The basic design principles that guide the development of websites for children and adults lead to many other topics, such as navigation, content, design continuity, and readability. Those topics, as they relate to designing for kids, are discussed in more detail later in this chapter.

Focus on Content

It is sufficient to say that if a website designed for children lacks content and appeal, it will not be used by kids. Children are no dummies. They can spot a poorly designed site that lacks any original content or activities for them from a mile away. Just like adults, they are inclined to go to sites that speak directly to their interests and spark their attention rather than to sites that try to do too much for too many different audiences.

Focused content has a strong influence on children and their attitudes toward your website. The topics you include, the depth in which you deal with them, and the way in which they are presented all play a critical role in how a child views and interacts with your site. A 2002 study of how children view and use websites found that children "knew exactly which content was hot for them and what was not." When children were asked how they decide where to go on a website, the most common reply was that they just "look around and see what's interesting." The content that the majority of kids found most interesting either addressed current children's trends (such as Harry Potter) or general children's interests (such as dinosaurs), or was the focus of a high-quality presentation ("It looked cool").[6]

Identify Your Audience

When developing content for kids, it is vitally important to keep in mind the specific age of the group you are trying to reach. Children, especially those elementary-school age and above, are very sharp computer users and are quick to decide whether a website's content is of interest to them. In just a few seconds they can also determine whether a site is intended for them or for a younger or older audience. Therefore it is important to ensure that your website makes a good first impression and speaks very clearly to the interests of your target age group.

If your library site is going to contain content, information, and activities for several different age groups, you might want to consider providing subcategories or adding a different entrance (section) for each age group to your main page. Many library sites already do this when they break out sections of their children's page for preschoolers, elementary-school students, middle-school students, and teens. However, it is important to go beyond merely labeling different sections of your site with age-related text headings; you also need to make sure that children can visually identify with the categories. How many first or second graders do you know who can spell "elementary"? If the page is designed to include meaningful images as part of its content, elementary-school children will be more successful in locating which part of the site is intended for them. Additionally, if you plan to include supplemental content for adults (parents, teachers, librarians), make sure to place it in a separate section or page and label it clearly (for example, "For Parents" or "Teachers Corner"). This will assist adults in locating the information that is intended for them and will avoid overwhelming children with a lot of potentially confusing text that will make it harder for them to navigate the site.

The home page for KidsLinQ, shown in Figure 3-2, is designed to appeal to the site's target age group and clearly identifies which section is for adults. KidsLinQ is a website designed by children's librarians for elementary-school children (aged 6 through 11 years). The home page of the site uses an uncluttered design with images that appeal to children and direct them toward common library resources they might be looking for. The site does a good job of targeting the age group that the library is trying to reach. Visual images help children identify the various types of activities found on the site, and simple words make the site easy to read. A small statement at the very bottom of the home page clearly summarizes the

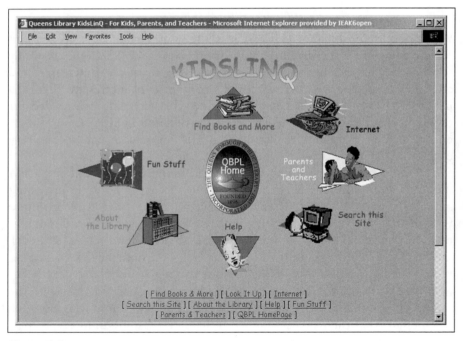

Figure 3-2
KidsLinQ Home Page (http://www.kidslinq.org), Queens Borough Public Library, Jamaica, New York

site's purpose and audience: "Find online tools and research resources for children between ages 6–11." Not overlooked is a separate section for parents and teachers that pulls together information resources pertaining to education, family diversity, getting ready for school, and the like.

Tap into Children's Natural Curiosity

Children are naturally curious, which can get them into trouble all the time. But that curiosity is also what fuels discovery, imagination, and learning, and is often what sets kids apart from many adults. The thirst for discovery and new experiences is one of the reasons the Internet is so attractive to children. The interactive nature of the Web not only allows children to explore other worlds and cultures (which books also do) but also enables them to connect and communicate with children from faraway places. Like a child's curiosity, the Internet has no boundaries or borders. Perhaps that is why children and the Internet go so well together.

In developing sites for children, it is important to tap into a child's natural curiosity by making your site not only a destination for curious minds but also a guide that encourages them to discover more. This is what many libraries attempt to do with children's web directory pages that provide links to fun sites for kids to explore. However, kids want more than simple links to suggested sites. They want activities that provide them with a challenge, an opportunity to prove their knowledge or skill, and the ability to explore and learn something new. Content that helps children tap into their naturally curious minds and share their knowledge with others has great appeal. Activities like Internet scavenger hunts, brain games, and creative writing journals score big with young users who enjoy stretching their minds. As you begin to develop a plan for building your library site for children, be sure to continually ask yourself, "How does this site and the activities it provides tap into a child's natural curiosity?" If you keep that question in mind, you will be well on your way to developing a site that appeals to kids.

Figure 3-3 illustrates a website that was designed to pique children's curiosity. This site, which was jointly created by the Public Library of Charlotte and Mecklenburg County and the Mint Museum of Art through a grant from the Institute of Museum and Library Services (IMLS), strives to provide children with a fun way of exploring traditional North Carolina crafts. The site was built not to supplement school curriculum guides but rather to offset the library's lack of printed material about the topic and to create an atmosphere that sparks children's curiosity to learn. With differ-

Figure 3-3
Hands on Crafts (http://www.handsoncrafts.org), Public Library of Charlotte and Mecklenburg County and Mint Museum of Art, Charlotte, North Carolina

ent sections of the site devoted to fiber and clay crafts, children can play around with a host of virtual activities, such as the Clay Lab, the Virtual Pot Throw, and Weave Wally a Wardrobe, that encourage them to explore. In addition to the engaging multimedia activities, children will also find video clips of kids their own age doing crafts and talking about how they got involved in weaving, basketry, pottery, and more. The site's design, colors, and whimsical navigation help to tap into a child's curiosity and make the site a fun destination for discovery and learning.

Be Fresh and Current

Keeping your site fresh and up-to-date is critical if you want children to return. In today's technology-driven world, children are accustomed to having access to information that is constantly updated, whether through school, on TV, or in other media. They assume that information that relates to their world will be current and, in many cases, real-time. The same holds true for children's interaction on the Web. After children have visited a site a few times, they expect to see that things have changed or that there is something new—an indication that the site is fresh. When the content remains the same or is flat, children become less likely to return to the site or to recommend it to other kids.

Keeping fresh and current content on your website can be challenging, but not if you share the burden of providing fresh content with other staff members and even with your users—the children. When designing your site, try to think of activities that would allow other members of your staff to contribute to the content or, even better, that would enable children to contribute to your site.

The BookHive web page in figure 3-4 illustrates how children may be encouraged to contribute to a site. One of the built-in functions of this site

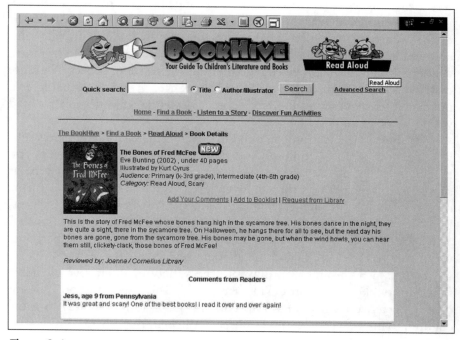

Figure 3-4

BookHive Comments from Readers (http://www.bookhive.org), Public Library of Charlotte and Mecklenburg County, Charlotte, North Carolina allows children to add their comments to reviews of books they like. The comments are reviewed periodically (twice a week or more) by a children's librarian on the BookHive team through a back-end interface that is used to edit (only if necessary) and tag comments for display. Once approved, the child's comment is added to the book review and to the rotation of comments that are displayed on the BookHive's home page. Additionally the site allows staff to highlight something different each month through its Zinger Recommends feature and to inform users of what is new under The Latest Buzz. Because the site's design is well thought out, updating content takes only a few minutes each month and uses a series of web forms that enable both staff and children (not familiar with HTML or any other web language) to provide the fresh content themselves.

Engage with Interaction

Interactive features on websites that allow users to voice their opinions or test their skills score big with kids who are starting to define their sense of identity. Features such as polls, opinion forms, quizzes, and image rollovers not only encourage children to interact with your site but also provide valuable content. Interactive elements and features do more than merely inform children about a topic, they engage them in the learning process. Because children learn best through hands-on experience, including some type of interactive element in your site's design is essential if you want to hold young users' attention.

The type of interaction you build in depends mainly on your site's subject area and depth of content. And the types of interactive elements you employ may be just as varied as your subject area. Interaction may be as simple as image rollovers that allow children to discover hidden elements on the screen or as complicated as allowing a child to carry on a conversation with a screen character or another child. No matter what type of interactive feature you choose to build, it is important to keep in mind both privacy issues (see chapter 4) and the learning objectives you wish to achieve.

Figures 3-5 through 3-8 illustrate the variety of interactive elements found on public library sites. Kidspace (figure 3-5) uses a fun poll among other interactive elements (choose Fun and Games on that site) to allow children to interact and express themselves through the site. OH! Kids (figure 3-6) engages children on its home page and throughout the site by using simple rollover animations that let users discover what the site has to offer. Potamus Place (figure 3-7) offers children lots of interaction and information through features such as Potamus's poll and animated e-mail cards. And the Florida Library Youth Program enables children to use input forms to have a conversation with Flyp, the program's mascot (figure 3-8).

Create Comfort

It is a well-known fact that children, especially young children, love characters. Perhaps it is because children can easily identify with the make-believe world that characters live in or because characters provide children with some level of comfort in new and unfamiliar environments. Either way, it is clear from an educational standpoint that characters aid young children in the learning process. "Giving children a character to identify with [helps] kids enjoy learning that much more," states Andrea Mulder-Slater, an educator and professional workshop leader. "Young children respond especially well to a character who is showing them new things. Good

Figure 3-5
Kidspace (http://www.cincinnatilibrary.org/kidspace), Public Library of Cincinnati and Hamilton County, Cincinnati, Ohio

content is very important, but it is not enough to simply offer information. That information must be delivered [to kids] in an interesting way."[7] Friendly characters help to do this.

As children's librarians we too are familiar with the important role of characters. Many libraries around the country have mascots or have built programs (such as summer reading) around friendly characters that engage children's interest and help them feel comfortable with libraries and all they have to offer. Characters on a website can do the same. Characters can be as simple as a smiley face or as elaborate as a whole cast of cartoon characters. The choice depends on who your target audience is and what the objectives of your website are.

Further studies show that allowing children some level of interaction with a character greatly enhances their learning experience and encourages them to explore more. The interaction could be as minimal as a simple mouse-over animation or as elaborate as a multimedia-enhanced dialogue

Figure 3-6
OH! Kids Home Page (http://www.oplin.lib.oh.us/products/oks), Ohio Public Library Information Network (OPLIN), Ohio

between a character and the child. A study in this area showed that children felt empowered by the ability to influence or control a character's action on the screen through the use of a mouse or keyboard. Furthermore, the interaction between character and child had other benefits. Children enjoyed having characters address them or ask them to perform tasks and were more likely to follow instructions when they were presented in a friendly and fun way.[8] Understandably, not every library system has the resources to create, or hire developers to create, characters who can interact with children through elaborate multimedia environments. But what is important to remember is that when you consider what content your site will contain, try to include some type of character (cartoon, real-life, abstract) that will help children feel comfortable. If children do not view your site as a friendly and fun place to explore, they will not use it.

Arlington County Public Library has had a Kids' Corner site since 1997. In the last few years the site has undergone several transformations,

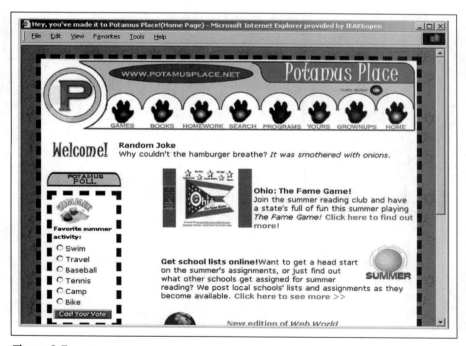

Figure 3-7
Potamus Place Home Page (http://www.potamusplace.net), Cleveland Heights–University Heights Public Library, Cleveland Heights, Ohio

making it what it is today. As illustrated in figure 3-9, the site's design relies heavily on a playful color scheme and creates a child-friendly environment by using colorful characters that kids can relate to. In almost every section of the site, you will find Cool Cat or one of his little mouse friends playfully helping children identify what is on the page. Under the Sports page, Cool Cat is displayed playing soccer; under the Homework page, he is up to his ears in books; and under the Storytimes page, he is sharing a book with his mouse buddies. In addition to Cool Cat, the site displays another character familiar to children and libraries that use TLC/CARL's Kid's Catalog. With Carl's permission, the library incorporated K.C., the Kid's Catalog mascot, into the design of its site. This friendly green robot strategically placed near the link to the Kid's Catalog helps children visually build a bridge between the Kid's Corner site and the library catalog. The site definitely offers much in the way of design, color, and characters to help a child feel at home.

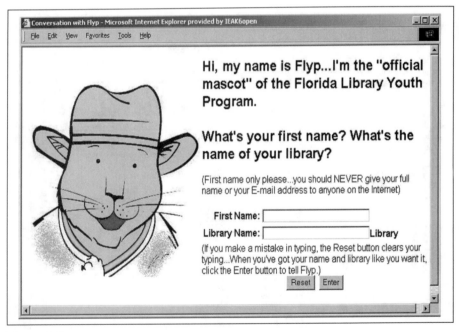

Figure 3-8
Conversation with Flyp (http://dlis.dos.state.fl.us/bld/flyp2002/TalkToFlyp/default.asp), Florida Library Youth Program (FLYP), State Library of Florida, Tallahassee, Florida

Figure 3-9
Kids' Corner Home Page (http://www.co.arlington.va.us/lib/kids), Arlington County
Department of Libraries, Arlington, Virginia

NAVIGATION GUIDELINES

When visiting a new website, children, like adults, feel most comfortable if
the navigation scheme for the site seems somewhat familiar. This familiarity can manifest itself in many ways. It may be that the category descriptors
are common and recognizable (About Us, Library Catalog, Search, etc.) or
that the layout of the navigation scheme is familiar (left sidebar or bar
across the top of the page). Specifically which elements are familiar is not
particularly important. What is important is that when children first visit a
website, they encounter some element of familiarity that assists them in fig-
uring out where to find the information they seek. For children, who are
natural seekers of information and knowledge, it is crucial to provide a navigation structure that immediately makes users feel comfortable.

Keep the Structure and Layout Simple

When developing a navigation scheme for a children's site, it is important not to dissect the information into too many categories and subcategories. A richly laid-out navigation structure that branches into many page levels tends to confuse children, who are not accustomed to having to click three and four times through several levels to locate what they are looking for. For the most part, this type of drill-down scheme does little more than ensure that children will never visit a site again—that is, unless the site includes a prominent search feature to help manage the navigation.

For younger children, the navigation scheme that seems to work best is one that includes no more than six or seven choices or categories. The use of visuals will further enhance the navigation scheme's usability. As stated before, visuals are very helpful in assisting children, and especially young children, in identifying what type of information they can find in your site. For instance, many sites commonly use a magnifying glass to indicate a search feature or a question mark to represent an "ask" feature or frequently asked questions (FAQ) list. Such graphic metaphors, along with descriptive text for each category, will assist children—especially those who are just beginning to develop reading skills—in navigating your site with ease.

Although the use of images in a site's navigation structure can be important for young users, it is not always necessary, especially if your target audience is upper-elementary- or middle-school-age children. Older children who can read well often need only category descriptions that they can understand and relate to. When creating category descriptions, it is best to be as concise as possible and to avoid using overly cutesy language. Older children, like adults, use their eyes to quickly scan a site's content and navigation structure to determine if the site contains the information they are looking for. When web developers try to get too colorful or too trendy with a site's language, they often drive away their intended audience. Labels like "Treasure Chest," "In the Know," and "Locker Room" do little to assist a student in determining what type of content can be found in those sections or on the site. According to children's user studies,[9] it is far better to employ simple and easy-to-understand language, such as "Homework Help," "Fun and Games," and "Books and Authors," to help children locate what they are looking for.

In addition to keeping the language simple, it is important to make the entire navigation structure easily viewable on the screen without forcing the user to scroll. If the navigation menu is not always easily visible within a standard browser window, some of your site's content may be rendered unusable, simply because children will not see it on the viewable screen. Most of today's websites are designed for optimal viewing at a 600 × 800 screen resolution or greater, which accommodates nearly 94 percent of computer users.[10] However, depending upon the configuration and age of your library's computers, you may want to develop and test your design at a 480 × 640 screen resolution, which was the long-time development standard in the 1990s. If your site's navigation structure is not fully accessible to the user within the viewable window, you may want to rethink it or come up with a new layout.

Finally, it is necessary to consider the use of white, or nonclickable, space in the layout of a site's navigation structure. Many websites for children use image maps that allow kids to click on a part of a picture or an image to enter a section of the site. This type of navigation structure works fine as long as the clickable area is well defined. However, image maps that are designed too tightly will often frustrate and confuse children, whose little hands are prone to click accidentally on the wrong space. When developing the layout and look of your navigation structure, make sure you allow plenty of room for a user to move freely around the screen between the navigation elements. Try not to create a site that looks crowded and confusing or that is hard for children to navigate.

Let Children Know Where They Are

When determining the navigation scheme for a site, second- and third-level pages should not be overlooked. Sometimes search engines, which spider for keyword content and placement on the page, pay more attention to secondary pages than to home pages. Consequently, children are very likely to stumble upon a site from a second- or third-level page before they view its home page. The first step in minimizing the potential for confusion is to ensure that the site's navigation structure is viewable on all pages within the site. The next step is to provide some type of indicator that lets children know where they are within the site.

There are a variety of ways to help children make this distinction. Adding a category heading to the top of each page is perhaps the easiest approach, but sometimes the composition of a page's content requires the use of other methods. Using a different background color for each section or identifying the category by a picture are two alternative ways of helping children know where they are within a site. The important thing is to keep your navigation scheme in mind as you design your entire site, not just as you design your home page.

The Ohio Public Library Information Network created a navigation structure that makes it easy for children to determine where they are within the OH! Kids site. Each of the four main category headings is identified on the home page through the use of a graphic and color-coded text. When a child clicks on a second-level page, not only is the graphic for that category shown in the page's upper left corner, but in addition, the entire background of the page changes to the same color as the text in the category name. For example, in the WebTots section, the background is red and a cute little teddy bear graphic can be found on all the pages. In the WebKids area, the background is green and the graphic is a friendly little dragon, as shown in figure 3-10. Incorporating color and engaging graphics into the navigation scheme of this site works well, especially for younger users.

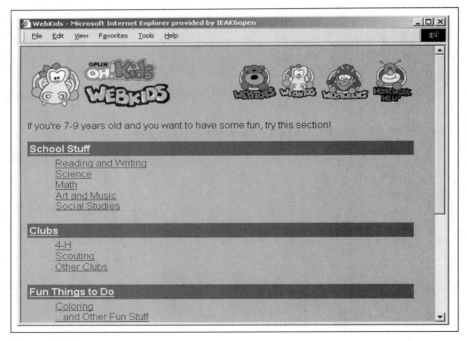

Figure 3-10
OH! Kids WebKids Color-Coded Page (http://www.oplin.lib.oh.us/products/oks), Ohio Public Library Information Network (OPLIN), Columbus, Ohio

Consider a Search Feature

If the site you are planning to build will contain a large amount of content, you will probably want to consider adding a feature that will allow children to search the site. Search boxes can be extremely helpful in locating information, especially for school-age children who use the computer for homework assignments and are familiar with how such finding aids work (and sometimes do not work). For sites that contain only a few pages, however, adding the ability to search is overkill. Additionally, the content of some kinds of sites, such as summer reading sites, does not merit the addition of a search function. The websites that benefit most from the addition of a search tool are those that contain a wealth of content. Homework-assistance sites, such as KidsClick (http://www.kidsclick.org), which contain hundreds of annotated, linked pages in dozens of categories, would be difficult for many students to use if they did not provide search tools.

If you do decide to integrate a search tool into the design of your site, be sure to make it part of your navigation scheme so that it is accessible from every page. Nothing is more frustrating than having to go searching for a site's search tool. If a search tool is not easily visible and accessible, the purpose of having one is defeated.

An example of an easy-to-use form for a search is shown in figure 3-11. Fundamental to the design of the BookHive book review site for kids is the search tool that allows users to easily locate books by title, author, illustrator, genre, and more. Since the site has grown in the past few years to well over a thousand reviews, the staff wanted to make sure that children would have an easy way to locate titles or authors of books they like. To accommodate this objective, the library added both quick and advance searching features to the site. Across the top of every page in the Find Books section of the site, children will find a search box that allows them to perform a quick search by either title or author/illustrator. In addition, children can use the advanced search feature to narrow their search by book audience (reading level), number of pages, reviewer (in case they want to find other books reviewed by a staff member they like), and recent publication dates. The search feature is one of the strongest, most user-friendly elements the site has to offer; without it, navigating the site's large amount of content might be a nightmare.

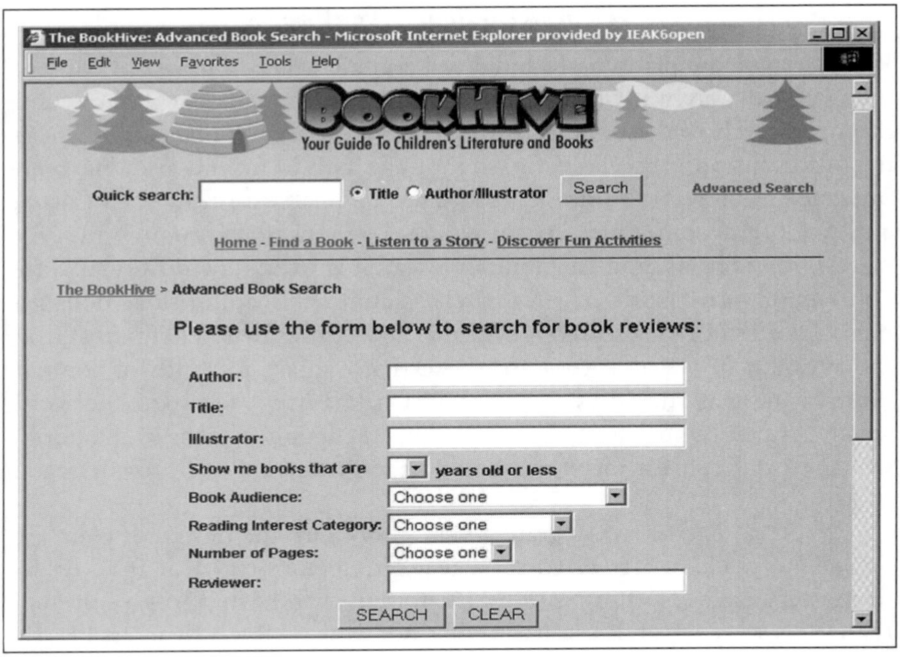

Figure 3-11
BookHive Search Form (http://www.bookhive.org), Public Library of Charlotte and Mecklenburg County, Charlotte, North Carolina

Do Not Mess with the Browser

With the growing concern about protecting children who use the Internet from accidentally being exposed to harmful material, some children's websites have gone as far as including scripts in their mark-up code that turn off or remove navigation elements from the browser window. Typically, these sites try to mimic what looks like a full screen mode. However, in reality, although they have removed access to all the usual navigation buttons in a browser window, they have not removed the potential dangers to the child. Removing the browser buttons forces children to figure out how to navigate back and forth between pages using only the site's navigation structure. Children, just like adults, are easily frustrated by this practice. And, no matter how good your intentions may be in controlling children's access to potentially harmful material, eliminating the browser buttons is never a good idea. Consider the child writing a short report about Maurice Sendak, his favorite author, for his fifth-grade English class. Using the library's Author and Books page, he locates and follows a link to a wonderful site, only to realize that he cannot find the site's web address to include in his bibliography. He asks his mother if she can help him, but she is equally frustrated because there is no address bar. Knowing that the site must be accessible through avenues other than the library's website, she opens a fresh browser and helps her son use a popular search tool, such as Google, to search for the site. Within a few minutes, she is successful in relocating the site and its web address. From this example, the boy learns that although the library's website made it easy for him to locate the author information he was looking for, it would not allow him to determine the site's address or where he was on the Internet. Thus, the next time he has a homework assignment that requires research, he will be more likely to use the search tool his mother showed him than to use the library's site.

MULTIMEDIA GUIDELINES

Children are easily drawn to sites that entertain them, and it is not hard to understand why. Things that move around the screen, audio that is amusing to the ears, and video that lets viewers in on the action are all fun activities that a child can experience when using a computer. Although many of these multimedia elements are designed only to add entertainment value to a website, it is a well-known fact that activities that engage the senses on many levels help to increase a child's ability to learn.[11]

Elements that engage, interact with, and entertain users are must-haves when you design a site for children. More than just the icing on the cake, such features are often what attracts kids to your site to begin with and what keeps them coming back and recommending the site to their friends. Word of mouth is a very powerful marketing tool, even among children, so making your site as appealing and engaging as possible is of paramount importance to ensure that young users will view your site as valuable.

Web developers have been adding multimedia elements to websites, especially those designed for children, for almost as long as the World Wide Web has been around. Simple elements such as animated GIFs were the first to take off in the early 1990s, followed closely by dynamic HTML, streaming video, Flash, and many other formats. Since many of the multimedia elements commonly used today (such as Flash, RealPlayer, and QuickTime) require a browser plug-in, it is important to practice good design manners when incorporating such elements into your site. Developers of multimedia components for the Web should take into consideration the new rules of etiquette described below.

Provide Download Information

The first and foremost rule of multimedia etiquette is to inform your users of expected download and play times. Children, just like adults, want to know what can be expected when they click on a link or object that is attached to a download. When download times, information about file sizes, or progression indicators are not built into multimedia components, children often become confused about where to go on the screen or how long to wait. As a result, they may often cut off or skip viewing an element and thereby miss the content on your site.

Keep Introductions Short

If incorporating Flash or some other popular multimedia application to provide an introduction for your site, be sure to keep the element short and entertaining. Children will be more likely to watch something short (5 to 10 seconds) than something that takes a while to load. Short download times are very important, especially on multimedia introductions, which serve as a child's first encounter with a site. First impressions are always important.

Provide Children with Control

Allowing children control over their environment is very important, especially on the computer. When creating multimedia components for your site, it is essential to keep that in mind. If your site includes a Flash introduction or other entertainment animation, be sure to allow users the option of skipping it. In many cases, users may be return visitors who have already seen the introduction and just want to get to the real content.

The idea of allowing children control over their online experience should be carried through to the development of the multimedia elements themselves. When creating stories, activities, or games, be sure that children have options that allow them to stop or pause within the activity. In activities for young children, it is useful to include an option that allows users to replay an animation or an activity sequence as well. In the end, anything you can do to increase children's ability to control their learning experience will add to the value that they find in your site.

For example, Start Squad, the State Library of North Carolina's portal, illustrated in Figure 3-12, gives children the option of viewing the site in either HTML or Flash. The Flash version includes the same content as the HTML version but also provides animated characters and a short introduction clip of "the very best place to start." The site's home page states this option very clearly and provides a link to the Flash player for users who do not already have it. The home page also includes a short, helpful guidance statement about the plug-in: "Make sure you ask your parents for assistance if you are not sure."

Figure 3-12
Start Squad Options for Viewing (http://www.startsquad.org), State Library of North Carolina, Raleigh, North Carolina

Use Passive Animation for Longer Downloads

If a multimedia component requires a download that may take longer than 30 seconds to retrieve, it is best to build in some type of passive animation. Providing an animated visual while the rest of the multimedia file loads helps to keep children interested and gives them something to focus on while they wait.

Figure 3-13 illustrates how a simple animation can be used to fill time while a download is retrieved. StoryPlace, an animated story and activity site for preschoolers, uses Macromedia's Flash player to deliver its multimedia content. Since many of the stories and activities can take up to two minutes to download on a very slow modem (28.8K), the Flash components are designed to include a small animation for children to view while the rest of the story or activity downloads. In this example, from the preschool library story *Morris's Special Day,* a friendly little bluebird flaps its wings to entertain young users while the rest of the story loads in the back-

Figure 3-13
StoryPlace Animated Loading Screen (http://www.storyplace.org), Public Library of Charlotte and Mecklenburg County, Charlotte, North Carolina

ground. The loading screen also informs the user of the approximate download time based on a slower modem.

Provide Plug-in Information

If the viewing of a multimedia element requires the installation of a plug-in on the user's computer, be sure to identify which plug-in is required and include a link to the site where it can be found. Developers often take this rule of etiquette one step further and build in software scripts that detect if a user's computer has the proper plug-in installed. If not, the user will be pointed to a location where the plug-in can be retrieved and installed. Some developers may even write scripts that automatically install the plug-in on the user's computer. However, this approach is never good. Users should always be given the option of installing the plug-in, but they should never be forced. Allowing users to control their environment is also a fundamental rule of multimedia etiquette.

Use Sound to Enhance the Experience

Be sure to consider how the addition of sound to your website will affect the learning experience. For example, background music that is too loud can be distracting. In contrast, a triumphant drum-roll played as positive feedback for a correctly answered question can be an enhancement. Obviously, the goal is to choose audio features that will be perceived as enhancements, not disruptions, especially by the children you are trying to reach.

One effective way to incorporate sound into a website is as a supplement to an animation or other visual. Sound by itself can be entertaining to some children, but sound that is designed to complement activities, images, and games will appeal to a broader audience.

Potamus Place, illustrated in figure 3-14, uses a variety of audio files to engage children in exploring its many sections. The navigation scheme is loaded with fun sounds that play when a mouse is moved over a heading. In addition, children are given the option of deciding whether they want to listen to background music or not. Those who do not enjoy the catchy background tune can simply turn it off, and if they change their minds, they can turn it back on. Giving children control over this element adds a nice touch, especially since the background music provides only entertainment value, not actual content.

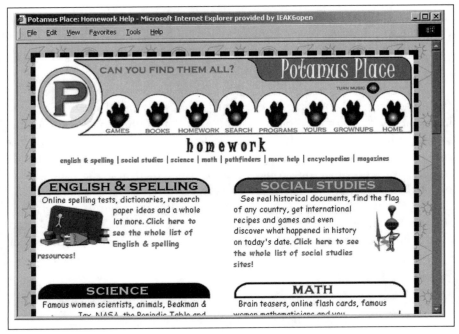

Figure 3-14
Potamus Place Navigation Scheme Incorporating a Variety of Sounds (http://www
.potamusplace.net), Cleveland Heights–University Heights Public Library, Cleveland
Heights, Ohio

MAKE LEARNING FUN

Although this chapter offers many guidelines, there is really only one fundamental principle to be kept in mind when developing library web services for children, and that is to *make learning fun.*

In the 1980s, during the pioneering days of multimedia design, Mark Lepper and Thomas Malone of Stanford University conducted and published several studies relating to computer multimedia and learning. The results of those studies have been published around the world and provide the foundation for many areas of multimedia instruction and design studied in colleges and universities today.[12] Similar research was conducted and published by Deborah Perry of Selinda Research Associates (http://www .selindaresearch.com) in the 1990s in regard to multimedia learning principles as they relate to intrinsically motivating museum experiences. Since libraries and museums share so much in common, it is easy to apply Perry's six components of learning to library websites and services as well.[13]

1. Curiosity: Does your website surprise or intrigue the user?
2. Confidence: Does your site help children feel safe and smart?
3. Challenge: Does your site encourage children to do or learn something new?
4. Control: Does your site help children feel in charge?
5. Play: Does your site encourage playfulness and exploration?
6. Communication: Does your site stimulate meaningful thought and conversation?

If you can keep those six components in mind when developing your library services for children, it should be easy to build a site that appeals not only to children but to people of all ages.

NOTES

1. Shuli Gilutz and Jakob Nielsen, *Usability of Websites for Children: 70 Design Guidelines* (Fremont, CA: Nielsen Norman Group, 2002), 4–5, http://www.nngroup.com/reports/kids.
2. Charles Flatter and Lynne S. Dumas, "Curiosity: Two to Five," Sesame Workshop, http://www.sesameworkshop.org/parents/advice/article.php?contentId=75001 (accessed January 19, 2004).
3. Irene C. Fountes and Gay Su Pinnell, *Matching Books to Readers in a Balanced Literacy Program* (Portsmouth, NH: Heinemann, 1999), 27.
4. Dina Demner, "Children on the Internet," April 2001, http://www.otal.umd.edu/UUPractice/children (accessed January 19, 2004).
5. Tim McDonald, "Study: U.S. Teens Are Generation 'IM,'" June 21, 2001, NewsFactor Network, http://www.newsfactor.com/perl/story/11444.html (accessed January 19, 2004).
6. Gilutz and Nielsen, *Usability of Websites*, 96.
7. Kim Wimpsett, "Building Websites for Kids," December 29, 1998, http://builder.com (accessed February 26, 2003).
8. Gilutz and Nielsen, *Usability of Websites*, 102.
9. Ibid., 62.
10. Merlyn Holmes, *Web Usability and Navigation: A Beginner's Guide* (New York: McGraw-Hill/Osborne, 2002), 139.
11. Lynn Stanley, "What Does Purple Smell Like?" *Childhood Education*, Summer 1997, 240.
12. T. W. Malone and M. R. Lepper, "Making Learning Fun: A Taxonony of Intrinsic Motivation for Learning," in *Aptitude, Learning and Instruction*, ed. R. E. Snow and M. J. Farr, vol. 3 of *Cognitive and Affective Process Analysis* (Hillsdale, NJ: Lawrence Erlbaum, 1987), 223–253.
13. Deborah Perry, "What Makes Learning Fun?" Selinda Research Associates, http://www.selindaresearch.com/learning.htm (accessed January 19, 2004).

CHAPTER 4

Special Considerations

S ome elements of web design, such as layout and content, are highly visible, while others, although they occur in the background, are crucial to a website's success and efficiency. Those background elements—the secret ingredients, you might say—make your site more palatable by addressing the accessibility and rights of young users and their families. This chapter will explore three areas—privacy, accessibility, and maintenance—and how their proper incorporation into your site's design helps users to take better advantage of the web service your library has developed.

PRIVACY: ISSUES AND GUIDELINES

Libraries have a responsibility to protect children while at the same time providing them with access to the information they need. As technology offers ever-increasing options for providing services to children, precautions must be taken to balance children's safety with the convenience of an online environment. A website designed specifically for children under 13 years of age should take great care to ensure the privacy of its users by not displaying personal information that could be used to trace or contact individuals. Information collected from children should be kept as basic as possible and should not go beyond what is necessary for the related activity. A library's guidelines for collecting and displaying children's information should be disclosed to the public so that adults will know what safeguards are in place to protect children's safety. Privacy issues are complicated, but they are as important as your site's content and technical considerations.

Children's Online Privacy Protection Act (COPPA)

Protecting the safety of children makes simple common sense for a library, but that is not always so for commercial ventures that host websites for children. Unfortunately, some commercial sites see no problem with collecting personal information from a child to use for marketing or other purposes. Protecting the anonymity of children is a good way to keep them from being targeted. Internet safety guides encourage caregivers, teachers, and librarians to teach children not to give out personal information while online. This includes information that may be requested in order to access a game or receive a special offer, although children may think such situations differ from telling a stranger about themselves in a chat room or e-mail.

To help regulate the way children's personal information is collected and used, Congress passed the Child Online Privacy Protection Act (COPPA), which went into effect in April 2000. The goal of COPPA is to put "parents back in charge of their children's personal information online."[1] The how-to and enforcement of COPPA is handled by the Federal Trade Commission (FTC), which designed the rules and guidelines that commercial sites for children must follow. COPPA applies to commercial websites whose target audience is children under 13 years of age or general-audience sites that knowingly collect personal information from children under 13 years of age. Operators of such sites must do the following:

Post a privacy policy explaining how a child's personal information is collected and used.

Notify parents and obtain consent before personal information is collected from a child.

Allow parents to choose whether to consent to the collection of personal information and provide them the option of prohibiting the disclosure of collected information to a third party.

Provide parents with access to their child's personal information to review or delete.

Maintain the confidentiality, security, and integrity of information collected.

Another significant condition set by the ruling is that a child's participation in an online activity cannot depend on his or her provision of personal information that is not required to perform the activity.

COPPA was designed primarily to address how commercial websites collect and use information from children. The ruling does not specifically address not-for-profit organizations, including libraries. However, that does not mean that libraries should not be informed of the guidelines. The American Library Association (ALA) strongly recommends that libraries follow COPPA guidelines.

Libraries also maintain the role of educating students and parents about COPPA's privacy options while a child is using the Internet either within a library or remotely. ALA has worked with the FTC from the beginning to determine the role of COPPA in an educational setting, which includes schools and libraries. ALA's recommendations regarding libraries and COPPA can be found at http://www.ala.org/coppafaq.

When applying general COPPA guidelines to the collection and use of children's personal information, the following individually identifiable information is to be avoided:

> **SOURCES OF INFORMATION ON COPPA**
>
> Children's Online Privacy Protection Act of 1998 (http://www.ftc.gov/ogc/coppa1.htm). The actual guidelines established in 1998 by the Children's Online Privacy Protection Act.
>
> Frequently Asked Questions on the Children's Online Privacy Protection Act (http:// www.ala.org/coppafaq). The American Library Association's information pages for libraries regarding COPPA.
>
> Kidz Privacy (http://www.ftc.gov/bcp/conline/edcams/kidzprivacy). The Federal Trade Commission's family-friendly site offering information for parents, teachers, media, businesses, and even kids regarding COPPA compliance and issues.

First and last name

Home or other physical address, including street name and name of city or town

E-mail address

Telephone number

Social security number

Any other identifier that enables physical or online contact with a child

Applying COPPA guidelines to your children's web service protects not only the privacy of the children using your site but also your library. Of course, many commercial children's sites do collect some personal information in order for a child to engage in the sites' activities. In such cases,

COPPA requires parental consent. Because public libraries do not operate for commercial purposes and therefore do not fall under the jurisdiction of COPPA, strict adherence to COPPA's rules is not required. Nonetheless, libraries should use COPPA guidelines as a model for their own privacy policies regarding the collection of children's personal information through the Internet. Fortunately, the COPPA guidelines contain several provisions and exceptions that address most of the reasons why libraries might need to collect personal information from a child.

There are many cases in which a library website may want or need to collect personal information about a child. To provide e-mail homework assistance and to register for an online summer reading program are two common instances. COPPA allows for such occurrences and waives the need for parental consent under the following conditions:

> The information is used to respond to a one-time request from a child and is neither used to reconnect with the child nor stored permanently in a retrievable form. This would apply to e-mail requests for homework assistance and the like.

> A child's information and a parent's online contact information are used for the sole purpose of contacting the parent to obtain parental consent. For example, if a library has online registration for its summer reading program, it may want to gather parents' e-mail addresses to alert them that their children have signed up.

> A child's name and online contact information (to the extent reasonably necessary to protect the safety of a child participant on the site) are not used to recontact the child or for any other purpose and are not disclosed on the site, if the operator uses reasonable efforts to provide a parent notice of the name and online contact information collected from the child.

Trying to apply all of COPPA's guidelines can be almost as hard as trying to decipher the text of the ruling. Therefore we will take a different approach and look at some typical online children's activities in which privacy issues addressed by COPPA might arise.

Protecting Privacy While Engaging Children

As libraries expand their online children's services, they will create tools that engage children in participatory activities. Such activities may vary from simple opinion polls that allow children to post their thoughts for others to see to sophisticated online summer reading programs that collect children's registration information and allow them to keep online reading logs. No matter what activities you consider adding to your children's website, it is important to keep children's safety in mind. Some ways in which libraries can integrate COPPA guidelines into the development of familiar types of online activities for children are examined below.

POLLS

An online poll collects and compares opinions on a topic. A poll topic and its results are usually displayed for only a short time and then are replaced with a new topic. Online polls can be kept completely anonymous simply by allowing children to select their answers from a list of options or can be personalized by providing children with the option of posting their comments. If a poll enables children to express their opinions in their own words, it makes sense to include the child's name, and perhaps age, as part of the online posting. Children enjoy seeing their names on-screen, and providing an activity that gives children a voice that can be shared with virtually anyone can be very appealing. A child's privacy can be guarded in an opinion poll if you are very specific about the information you request. There is no reason to gather a child's last name, home address, or e-mail address. Simply a first name, and perhaps age, should do. In fact, asking for a child's screen name can be equally effective and more anonymous. Figure 4-1 presents one example drawn from the many library sites offering kids' polls that do not require any identifiable personal information from a child.

BOOK REVIEWS

Book reviews, like polls, offer children a chance to voice their opinions. But unlike polls, which provide anonymity through consensus, book reviews enable children to publish their individual opinions. In activities that invite children to contribute reviews, online forms work well. The personal information that will be displayed about each child, the format of the review, and the search and navigation features of your site will help to determine what form fields to use. For example, if the purpose of your website is to bring together reviews from many countries, it would be logical to ask for the name of a reviewer's country. Such information is broad enough to be safely combined with a child's first name. Or if users will be able to search the reviews by parameters, such as reviewer's age or state, that information should be requested on the form. In any case, be sure to use the "least is best" rule when gathering personal information about a child. Do not ask

Figure 4-1
Kidsite Poll (http://www.montgomerycountymd.gov/Apps/Libraries/kidsite/
funstuff.asp), Montgomery County Public Libraries, Rockville, Maryland

for information that you do not intend to use, and never ask for more information than you need in order to allow a child to participate with a reasonable amount of anonymity.

Figures 4-2 and 4-3 show two online forms that enable children to share their opinions about books while divulging little or no personal information. The BookHive form (figure 4-2) allows children to add comments about books reviewed by library staff. Children do not need to provide details about the book itself, such as title and author, because their comments will be connected with the information already listed. The form asks only for first name, age, and state. The child's actual comments appear in a separate field. All children's personal information and comments are reviewed by staff before posting, and any personal references or information beyond that requested is edited out. This approach helps the staff to ensure that nothing personally identifiable is posted and enables them to check for inappropriate responses.

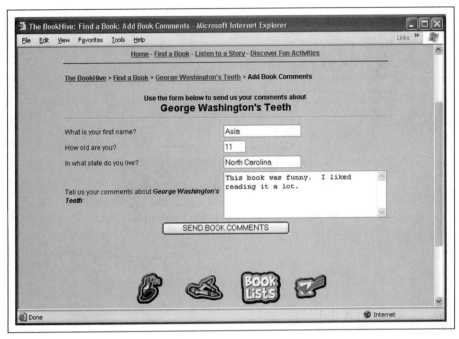

Figure 4-2
BookHive "Add Book Comments" Form (http://www.bookhive.org), Public Library of Charlotte and Mecklenburg County, Charlotte, North Carolina

The KidLinks site (figure 4-3) collects book reviews without requesting any personal information so that there are no privacy issues at all. The review form asks only for the book author and title, the review, and a rating of one to five stars. Brief guidelines on how to write a review (number of sentences, capitalization, and so forth) are displayed with the submission form. The form suggests checking for new review postings on Wednesdays and Fridays.

REGISTRATION

Although both polls and reviews collect personal information to support a child's comments, identifying the child is a secondary consideration. However, identification becomes the primary objective when personal information is collected for registration purposes. Registering children for library programs (such as summer reading) has a long tradition in public

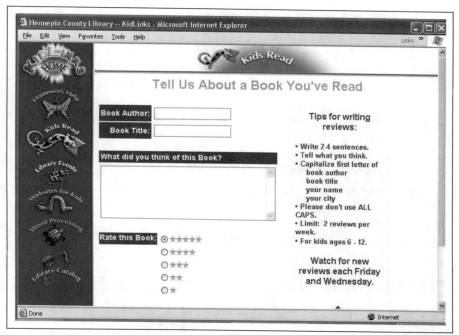

Figure 4-3

KidLinks "Tell Us About a Book You've Read" Form (http://www.hclib.org/kid/
frame.cfm?frame=kids_read.cfm), Hennepin County Library, Minnetonka,
Minnesota

libraries. Nonetheless, using technology to allow children to register online
is a fairly new practice—and a practice that requires particular attention to
safety. Although many registration forms request detailed information
about a child for statistical purposes, that information need not be displayed. The main concern when using online registration forms is to make
sure that the information is stored securely.

The benefits of an online registration system are many: children can
easily register from any location that provides Internet access (library or
home), libraries can access up-to-date information about a program's number of participants, and collecting statistical information about a program's
impact becomes a breeze.

Adding online components such as reading logs or other individual
activities is simplified if the framework of online registration (that is, a database) is already in place. As with other design decisions, looking at both the

current and the possible future uses of a child's information can determine what specifics are requested. If the goal is to offer online registration as an alternative to traditional registration, both methods should request the same information, such as name, grade, and library card number. If your library plans to send e-mail reminders about the program, then an e-mail address (preferably a parent's) should also be requested. Figure 4-4 shows the simple registration form developed by the Palo Alto Public Library for its 2003 summer reading program.

PERSONALIZED SITES AND PORTALS

Another reason information may be collected from a child is to personalize a site. The end result of the personalization process may take the form of an account that is employed to access a user-specified set of information or temporary, unstored information that is used to create a personalized inter-

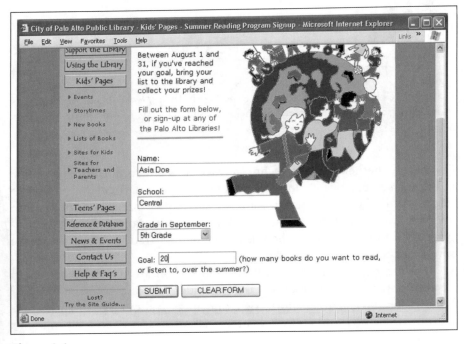

Figure 4-4
Online Registration Form for Summer Reading Program (http://www.city.
palo-alto.ca.us/palo/city/library/kids-teens/srpsignup.html), City of Palo Alto
Public Library, Palo Alto, California

active experience. Simplicity is still the major guideline for achieving the result with as little disclosure as possible. Personalization does not necessarily mean the collection of personal information. It means tailoring each child's online experience to him or her as an individual.

As discussed in chapter 2, portals offer a way for users to create a personalized site by maintaining an account that lets them set parameters. A library card may be necessary to determine user privileges, and an optional e-mail address may be requested to facilitate the sending of updates. However, personal contact information (first and last names, address) should not be required for creating an account. The purpose of portal accounts, like other activity accounts, is to allow users to access information that is unique to them and is therefore user-centered, not library-centered. Portal accounts can be managed anonymously with unique IDs or passwords, and should not be viewed as an opportunity to collect demographic information about children.

A good example of a personalized portal site that allows children to customize their access and online environment while still maintaining a high level of anonymity is Brarydog, the homework assistance site developed by the Public Library of Charlotte and Mecklenburg County. The form for creating a user ID and password for that site is presented in figure 4-5. The fields in that form do not ask for information that personally identifies a child. The only required user-specific pieces of information are user ID, password, greeting name (which can be a screen name), and zip code. Zip codes are used to verify users' log-in information when passwords are forgotten. Each child selects a unique user ID and password to be used to access his or her personal page. The greeting name is used by Brarydog himself—a friendly blue prairie dog—to greet the child at the beginning of each site visit. The e-mail address is optional and is used by the library only to inform users about updates to the site. The actual amount of personal information collected is minimal, but *personalization* is maximal.

PERSONALIZING A ONE-TIME ACTIVITY

Some online activities can be enhanced so that they are personalized just for the duration of the activity. In such cases—for example, the use of a personalized greeting—individual information is requested and used only until the child finishes the activity. The information is never stored in a database; it exists in the computer's memory merely for the duration of the activity. The State Library of Florida's Conversation with Flyp activity (figure 4-6) employs this approach. Throughout the activity, the child is prompted for

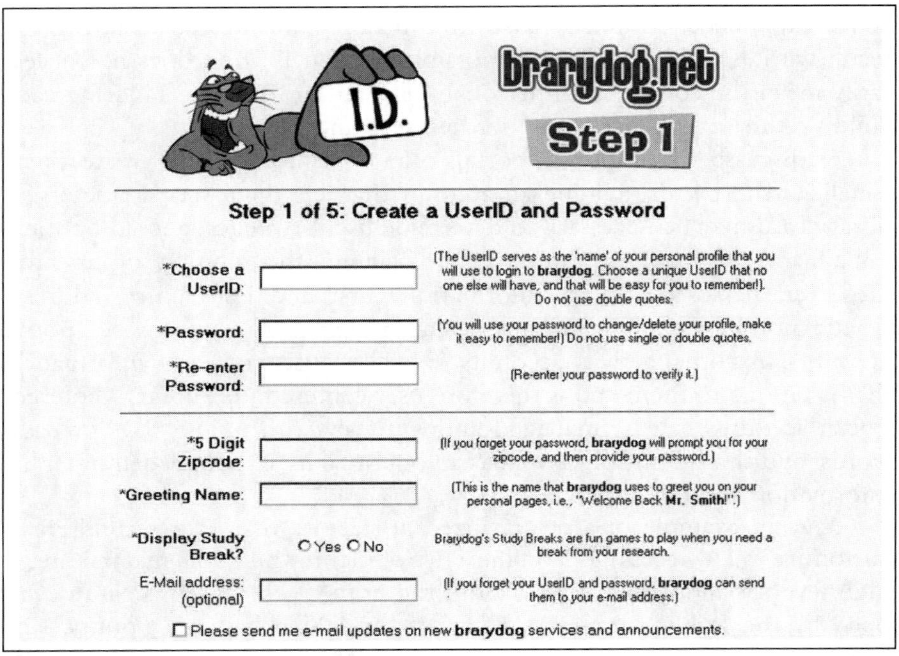

Figure 4-5
Brarydog Form for Creating a User ID and Password (http://www.brarydog.net),
Public Library of Charlotte and Mecklenburg County, Charlotte, North Carolina

name, library, and age. Flyp then uses that information to carry on a personalized conversation with the child. Conversation with Flyp is a good example of an online activity that personalizes a child's experience without raising privacy and safety issues.

REFERENCE

Providing a homework assistance or reference service via e-mail necessitates garnering enough information from children to respond to their queries. COPPA views this use of personal information as an exception, stating that parental consent to collect personal information is not needed when that information is used to respond directly on a one-time basis to a specific request. Multiple communications with a child about the same request are also deemed acceptable, although reasonable attempts should be made to contact the parents to let them know what information was collected and how it is used.

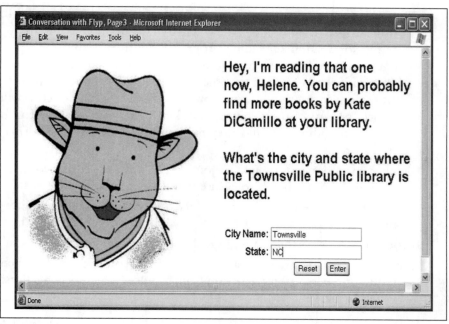

Figure 4-6
Personalized Conversation with Flyp (http://dlis.dos.state.fl.us/bld/flyp/talktoflyp/
default.asp), Florida Library Youth Program (FLYP), State Library of Florida,
Tallahassee, Florida

No matter what personalized activities your library may offer on its
children's website, the following tips can help you to ensure the safety and
privacy of each child's personally identifiable information.

Allow children to use anonymous screen names whenever possible.

When developing personalized activities, try not to store information on
the computer. Instead, use temporary memory to enable children to
personalize their experiences without infringing on their privacy.

Never ever display a child's last name, address, or other personalized
information on your website. If you have activities that ask children
to supply identifying information for potential display on a page
(for example, in a book review form), be sure that staff are able to
review the information before it is posted. Even though a form may
ask only for a child's first name, some children may also give their
last names.

When children must supply a great deal of personalized information in order to participate in a library activity (for example, when registering for a summer reading program), consider asking for a parent's e-mail address so that you can generate an automatic e-mail notification letter saying that the child has signed up to participate and identifying the information you have collected. This will inform parents of their children's online activity and allow them to contact the library should they not want their children's information stored.

If your site recommends or links to commercial websites, be sure to check each site's privacy policy to ensure that it complies with COPPA.

Always delete and remove access to an activity's database (such as a summer reading registration database) once the activity is completed.

If your site displays a child's photograph, be sure to get parental consent.

Always ask for the smallest amount of information possible when requesting personal information from a child. Remember the "least is best" rule.

Developing safety features and incorporating them into your site's design can sometimes require extra effort. However, that effort is well spent if it ensures children's privacy.

Handling Photographs and Images

Like a giant scrapbook, the Internet offers many opportunities to share activities that take place within the physical library. It is appropriate for library websites to display images of children's artwork, poetry, and stories, and even photographs of children involved in library activities. However, including such elements requires additional considerations. It is strongly recommended that a signed parental release form be obtained for each photograph of a child (and child-created work) before it is displayed online. In addition, you will want to be particularly careful not to provide information that when combined with a photograph could enable contact with a child. To avoid potential problems, use first names only and add the first letter of a last name only when necessary. Under no circumstances should a photo of a child's face appear on your site unless a signed parental release form has been obtained.

If your library has a public relations or communications specialist, check with him or her to see if a parental release form already exists. If there is such a form, make sure that it covers Internet usage. If you need to cre-

ate a form, you may want to pattern it after the forms available on the following libraries' websites:

Mid Hudson Library System, Poughkeepsie, New York (http://mid
hudson.org/news/picturereleaseform.htm). Developed primarily
to address the use of photographic images, the library's simple
form specifically addresses the use of photos on the Internet.

North Suburban Library System, Wheeling, Illinois (http://www
.nsls.info/marketing/photo.html). The site provides several examples of parental release forms from other libraries.

Boston Public Library, Boston, Massachusetts (http://www.bpl.org/
teens/xtreme/regform.htm). In a web page created for its teen
program, BPL combines a parental release form with a registration
form, thus killing two birds with one stone.

Privacy Policy

A good way both to formalize your library's privacy guidelines and to notify
users about how you are safeguarding them is to write and post a privacy
policy. In addition to informing the public about the privacy provisions that
are in place in your library, the policy can serve as a guide to protecting
users' privacy during your site's development. The policy may be broad in
scope, addressing not only website-related issues but also traditional privacy
issues, such as the safeguarding of personal library card information and the
confidentiality of patron records.

ALA's Office of Intellectual Freedom has prepared a document entitled
"Guidelines for Developing a Library Privacy Policy," finalized in August
2003, that covers the topic well (http://www.ala.org/Template.cfm?
Section=Privacy1&Template=/ContentManagement/ContentDisplay.cfm
&ContentID=40426). This guide defines personally identifiable information (PII) and offers a structure for how to protect it. The guidelines also
suggest drafting a policy that addresses the five key areas of privacy: notice,
choice, access, security, and enforcement. Links to existing privacy policies
are provided and an appendix contains a good example of a library privacy
policy. Also included are a checklist of questions to ask as a policy is developed and a guide to how to conduct a privacy audit. Of special interest is a
section titled "Library Services to Minors," which addresses children's privacy issues and COPPA. ALA makes the following recommendations
regarding COPPA: "When a library designs web pages and services for chil-

dren, it may wish to provide the same privacy protections as the protections mandated for commercial websites."

Your library's privacy policy should be highly visible and easy to find on your website. Most library sites tend to include a link to this information somewhere on their home page, but to make the information accessible from anywhere within your site, we would suggest including a link at the bottom of each page. Here are some examples of library privacy policies that address COPPA concerns:

Carnegie Library of Pittsburgh, Pittsburgh, Pennsylvania (http://www.clpgh.org/about/privacypolicy.html)

Public Library of Charlotte and Mecklenburg County, Charlotte, North Carolina (http://www.plcmc.org/aboutUs/policiesPrivacy.htm)

Indianapolis Marion County Public Library, Indianapolis, Indiana (http://infozone.imcpl.org/kids_about_disclaimer.htm)

Liverpool Public Library, Liverpool, New York (http://www.lpl.org/AboutLPL/Policies/privacy.html)

ACCESSIBILITY: CLEARING THE WAY TO THE TABLE

It does not matter how tantalizing a meal is if the door to the dining room is locked. If content and format help to create the recipe for a site, accessibility options provide the utensils that allow users to partake of the feast. You would not provide a fork for eating soup or a butter knife for eating spaghetti. A good host anticipates a guest's needs, offering not only a fork for spaghetti, but also a spoon to accommodate both twirlers and non-twirlers. Similarly, not everyone who visits a website views the information in the same way. Individuals may have disabilities that prevent them from navigating the screen, reading or understanding text, or even using the computer in the same way as others. Visual, motor, auditory, and cognitive disabilities can affect how a user interacts with your website. A website is deemed accessible only when all users can experience, understand, and use the information presented despite any physical disabilities they may have.

Over 15 percent of online users have some type of disability (750 million people worldwide, 54 million Americans).[2] This number is more than significant enough to warrant attention. But even if the number were only 5 percent or less than 1 percent of the population, ensuring that a website is equally accessible to all users is fundamental to the founding premise of all libraries: to provide free and equal access to information and resources.

Accessibility Standards

Like privacy, the issue of accessibility is crucial and complicated. Therefore guidelines have been established to help developers understand how to create websites that accommodate all potential users, regardless of their abilities. There are two major sets of accessibility standards, the Web Content Accessibility Guidelines (WCAG) written by the World Wide Web Consortium's (W3C) Web Accessibility Initiative (WAI) and the Section 508 guidelines of the Rehabilitation Act Amendments of 1998. Section 508 compliance is currently required only for websites created by the federal government, but some state legislation may require compliance for state-funded agencies as well.

The Web Content Accessibility Guidelines are much broader in scale and have become the accessibility bible for web developers in building sites that are accessible to all. The WCAG provides a set of accessibility guidelines with multiple priority levels of compliance and an emphasis on those checkpoint components that provide the most access to the most users. There are three priority levels, each with its own set of checkpoints, that clearly define what a website needs to do to ensure accessibility.[3]

> **Priority 1.** Checkpoints *must* be met. Without these compliance elements, access may be impossible for some individuals. Satisfying Priority 1 checkpoints is a basic requirement for some groups to be able to use web documents.
>
> **Priority 2.** Checkpoints *should* be satisfied. Without these compliance elements, complete access to some components of the website may be difficult for some individuals. Satisfying Priority 2 checkpoints will remove significant barriers to accessing web documents.

ACCESSIBILITY RESOURCES

Web Accessibility Initiative (http://www.w3.org/wai). The World Wide Web Consortium's home for all issues dealing with accessibility. The site contains extensive information about guidelines, priority levels, checklists for developers, discussions, and more.

Federal Government Section 508 Guidelines (http://www.section508.gov). The federal government's home for all Section 508 accessibility issues.

Bobby (http://bobby.watchfire.com). Watchfire.com's well-known software tool that allows users to test web pages for compliance with WAI or Section 508 guidelines. Also provides good discussion of accessibility issues.

WAI Guidelines versus Section 508 (http://www.washington.edu/accessit/articles?18). From the National Center on Accessible Information Technology in Education, this section of the site provides a good overview of each set of guidelines as well as a side-by-side comparison of the two.

Priority 3. Checkpoints *may* be met. Without these compliance elements, complete access to some components of the website may be somewhat difficult for some individuals. Satisfying Priority 3 checkpoints will improve access to web documents.

Your library's web development policy should dictate at least a Priority 1 level of compliance, with the format and design of your site (such as tables, forms, frames, and applets) further defining any additional Priority 2 or 3 compliance options that may be needed. Although future changes and updates are inevitable in any web project, developing a site with accessibility elements in place from the beginning can prevent extensive redesign later. A complete checklist for all WCAG checkpoints at all priority levels can be found on the W3C WAI site.

A website that is accessible to all users need not be boring, lifeless, or completely text-based. Fortunately, adaptive and assistive computer technologies have come a long way in recent years in recognizing and handling images, navigation elements, and multimedia components. The guidelines outlined by W3C address such common website elements and thus allow the building of children's websites that are engaging, appealing, and enjoyable to all users.

BASIC COMPLIANCE

Basic compliance with the WCAG means that all checkpoints within the Priority 1 guidelines are met without exception. Without compliance at this level, your site or some elements within it may be inaccessible to some individuals with vision or motor disabilities. Satisfying all checkpoints at this level will remove significant barriers to accessing web documents and ensure that your site is in compliance.

The WCAG checklist provides detailed specifications for Priority 1 requirements. One approach many web developers use is to attack each checkpoint in order. However, Thomas Dowling,[4] the author of *The Library Web Manager's Handbook,* suggests grouping the checkpoints into four steps.

Four Easy Steps to a Mostly Accessible Website

1. Provide appropriate text alternatives for every nontext element on the site (WCAG guideline 1; 508 provisions A and I). Create text alternatives that allow users to understand what they would see if

they could view an image. If the nontext element is a hyperlinked image, the alternative text should tell users where the link will take them. If the nontext element is an audio or multimedia file, the alternative text should identify what the element is.

2. Use honest markup for document structure. If you use style sheets, make sure they are appropriate, with relative units of measurement for presentation. Check that the site is readable and accessible without its style sheet applied (WCAG guideline 3; 508 provision D). Tables, quotations, and other features should be used only to present specific information in a certain way, not as tools for indentation or other page layout features. With few exceptions, most screen readers see a table as an informational element and will not recognize a table if it is used otherwise. Absolute measurements can prevent a browser from adjusting fonts and other settings, which prevents a user from resizing a page for easier reading.

3. Use color to communicate information only in conjunction with textual clues (WCAG guideline 2; 508 provision C). Do not rely solely on color to indicate directions, navigation schemes, or other informational elements. Users who are color-blind may not be able to differentiate colors, and users who cannot see will be completely excluded. An exception would be activities designed to teach colors, in which case the selection of a color becomes the goal, not an instruction.

4. Avoid anything that blinks (WCAG guideline 7; 508 provision J). Blinking objects are not only indiscernible to users without sight but also, at certain rates (between 2 and 59 times a second), can cause seizures for some users with epilepsy. Leaving out any blinking images is the safest way to avoid this potential danger.

ABOVE AND BEYOND BASIC

Since most websites offer more than basic services, more than basic compliance is recommended. Sites that are complex tend to offer navigation features, tables, forms, and activities that require plug-ins. Many such elements are important in the development of websites for children because they offer high levels of interactivity. Sites that truly engage children often provide multimedia elements, sound, streaming video, and the like, and are graphic-intense. If your children's site will fall into that category, a more advanced level of compliance is recommended. Dowling recommends taking the following four steps to enhance your site's accessibility.[5]

Four Slightly Less Easy Steps to Nearly Complete Accessibility

1. Provide "skip navigation" options (508 provision O). To facilitate navigation, a row of links to various parts of a site is often located at the top or side of a web page. Most users can tune out such navigation bars until they are needed, but a screen reader would read each navigation bar on each page before getting to the main content. Consequently, to increase accessibility, it is important to provide the option of skipping navigation bars so that users of screen readers can proceed to the main information on a page in much the same way as any other user would.

2. Use tables correctly for tabular information (WCAG guideline 5; 508 provisions G and H). Screen readers analyze data in the order of its HTML source. This is called linearizing. Creating tables that identify headers for rows and columns lets a screen reader correctly interpret a cell by associating it with the proper information. For example, a table showing branch hours for several libraries should be set up with code for columns showing days of the week, then rows for branch names, followed by the times for each branch. Tables set up in this way will look the same as other HTML tables but will provide clarity that would otherwise be unavailable to users of screen readers.

3. Make information and navigation provided by client-side scripts or plug-ins accessible to users with screen readers, users with alternative input devices, and users with scripting disabled (WCAG guidelines 6 and 8; 508 provisions L and M). To meet this guideline requires either linking to a plug-in version that meets accessibility requirements, linking to a page that is accessible, or ensuring that a page works without plug-ins or scripts (such as Java). In other words, a user should be able to access the information presented without any bells and whistles.

4. Provide textual clues for all information requested in forms (WCAG guideline 12; 508 provision N). Much as proper coding helps screen readers decipher tables, providing textual clues in forms helps screen readers tell their users what information an input field is requesting. Textual clues not only help users but also ensure that the proper information will be entered into a form's underlying database.

Priority 2 compliance ensures that most users will be able to take advantage of most of a site's features. To make a site even more accessible, there is a third level of compliance that addresses some of the same issues as Level 2 but with different specifications. Many of the Level 3 guidelines deal with how assistive technologies interact with various aspects of a website, such as forms. Priority 3 guidelines, although important, are deemed less critical because the majority of users would still be able to retrieve information from sites that are not in compliance. For further information on Level 3 compliance, please refer to the Checklist of Checkpoints for WCAG at http://www.w3.org/TR/WCAG10/full-checklist.html.

Section 508 Guidelines

Although the WCAG are the industry standard, libraries should also be familiar with the federal government's Section 508 guidelines. The WCAG are recommended for noncommercial sites, whereas Section 508 is governing law for federal government websites. Most libraries are not mandated to follow Section 508, but it is good for librarians to recognize the similarities and differences in the two sets of guidelines. Section 508 outlines 16 website guidelines that must be followed in every federal government website (Internet and Intranet). Nearly all of the Section 508 guidelines are covered under the WCAG, and although in some cases the two sets of guidelines are identical, there are a few areas in which they differ. Several WCAG Priority 1 checkpoints (1.3, 4.1, 6.2, and 14.1) are not addressed in Section 508, for the most part because the government felt that they were not clear enough to identify an explicit course of action or that they were unenforceable (and therefore could not be laws). A few of the Section 508 guidelines are actually more restrictive than the WCAG and involve the use of flicker elements (flashing text, images, or screen) and scripting languages on a website. For more information about Section 508 and the differences and similarities between these two sets of guidelines, see

Federal Government Section 508 Guidelines (http://www.section 508.gov), which is the federal government's home for all Section 508 accessibility issues

JimThatcher.com Accessibility Consulting (http://www.jimthatcher .com/sidebyside.htm), which provides an excellent side-by-side comparison of the two sets of guidelines from both perspectives

When choosing a set of guidelines to ensure that your children's website is accessible, you will probably want to stick with the WCAG outlined by the W3C. Those guidelines are slightly broader in scope and address a few issues that Section 508 does not.

Verifying Accessibility

When creating an individual page for a website, a good developer constantly checks the browser window to make sure that the intended content is indeed being displayed. The developer will also constantly check accessibility elements to ascertain that they have been properly implemented. This can be done either manually or by using tools designed to check for and correct noncompliance. When testing accessibility compliance, a developer needs to use a variety of methods to confirm that all goals have been accomplished. A little effort can go a long way toward guaranteeing that your site will be used by as many children as possible, regardless of ability. (See chapter 7 for a detailed discussion of website-testing techniques.)

MAINTENANCE

The process of maintaining a site begins long before the site is ever unveiled. Determining what maintenance issues your site may entail should be part of your planning process, as well as determining who will be responsible for dealing with them. Maintenance issues can even influence decisions on what type of content to include, depending on whether staff is available to devote time and effort to keeping the content fresh. A link-heavy site could easily get in trouble if no one is checking the validity of the links or updating them, and a book review site could lose repeat visitors if new reviews are not added often. Maintaining a website is like dealing with leftovers: you must either keep the content fresh, find new uses for it, or throw out what is no longer needed. Since maintenance is the area that people most often forget about and fail to plan for, many sites become stale and unusable within a short amount of time. Like other background activities, proper maintenance keeps a site vital and gives users reasons to return.

Libraries are places of constant change, and their websites should reflect that. Nowhere is this truer than in children's services. Not only can dynamic content keep children and their families informed about current happenings in the library, but it can also entertain children with changing activities, information, and features. The only way to keep the content on your site fresh and current is with well-planned maintenance. Planning for maintenance and building interfaces that allow you to update content on your website can be easier than you might think. There are three steps in maintaining a website:

1. Create a maintenance plan. Think of the plan as the maintenance blueprint for your site.

2. Build maintenance interfaces. Provide forms, databases, and tools that make it easy for staff to update content. Children will not see most of this, but they will see the results.
3. Update the site. Consistently perform the actual maintenance after the site is live and follow through with the steps in your maintenance plan.

The overall goal of a strong maintenance plan is to outline the process of refreshing your website. Streamlining the process by using maintenance interfaces and tools to assist with time-consuming but necessary tasks will result in a fresh children's site. Not only will this approach help your staff to keep the content fresh, but it will also help to draw young users back again and again.

Developing a Maintenance Plan

When you develop a website you determine what your site will offer users and how it will deliver those offerings. The creation of a maintenance plan enhances the overall development process both by identifying issues that will affect content and technical management and by specifying solutions for the issues. Some sites naturally have more maintenance requirements than others. The more ephemeral a site's content, the more numerous the maintenance issues. That does not mean that libraries should avoid developing sites that are complex; they just need to plan for the maintenance that will be involved in supporting them.

Once you have established the basic concept for your site and made decisions about its structure (such as static versus dynamic information), you can identify issues involved in maintaining the site. When you develop a website maintenance plan, you are basically creating a task list that will be used throughout the life span of your site. The plan helps you anticipate and answer questions about what needs to be done, who will take care of it, and how it will be accomplished. The challenge of determining what needs to be done and when it will be done can be tackled while developing a maintenance plan. Here is a four-step process for developing a maintenance plan:

1. Identify site elements that will require maintenance or future enhancements.
2. Identify the updating issues for each element (what needs to be updated, how frequently, and so forth).
3. Identify the tasks required to deal with each maintenance issue and who will take responsibility for each task.
4. Determine if tasks can be streamlined through the development of a maintenance interface.

IDENTIFYING MAINTENANCE ELEMENTS

Most maintenance issues tend to fall into three main categories: content, communication, and technical. Determining which elements of your site fall into each category is an excellent way to identify areas that will require ongoing maintenance. This step does not address specific tasks; it only identifies areas that might need maintenance or follow-up.

Table 4-1 shows how some common website elements fit into the three categories. It illustrates how common website components, such as hyperlinks, can be separated from the big picture. Examining website elements one at a time makes it easier to determine what maintenance needs to be addressed. In addition, the categorization process helps to identify not only obvious elements but also more obscure ones (such as user feedback). Once all elements are identified, the actual maintenance issues connected to them can be determined.

IDENTIFYING INDIVIDUAL MAINTENANCE ISSUES

It is likely that many elements within your site will have one or more maintenance issues. For example, if your website will allow children to input comments about books they have read, you will more than likely want a member of your staff to review the comments before they are posted to your site. As you think through how this would be done, you will begin to identify the maintenance issues that are involved. In this case, the issues

WEBSITE MAINTENANCE CATEGORIES	SAMPLE ELEMENTS
Content	Hyperlinks Ongoing content updates 　　Book reviews 　　Calendar of events 　　Activities User input 　　Book reviews 　　Polls
Communication	E-mail or other user feedback
Technical	Code and script

Table 4-1
Website Maintenance Categories and Sample Elements

would relate to the ability to screen all submitted comments and approve them before posting on the site. You may decide that you also want the ability to edit the comments, which would raise yet another issue that your maintenance routine would need to address.

Another common maintenance issue involves the validity of hyperlinks within your site. How to make sure that links are valid and updated (with the correct URL added or the link deleted) is indeed a maintenance issue that needs to be addressed. Another, separate issue relates to the expansion of the existing set of links to include new sites. Table 4-2 outlines some common website elements and the maintenance issues involved with them. Several of the issues in the table are not straightforward and deserve some

WEBSITE ELEMENT	MAINTENANCE ISSUE
Hyperlinks	How will future updates be done? How and with what frequency will links be checked? Will new links be added?
User Input	Will a staff member screen user comments before posting? Is editing a feature that needs to be included? Do users need to know their input has been received?
Content Updates	What content will require updating? What will be the frequency of updating? Who will be responsible for updating? Who will double-check the updates? Is the content arranged in a standard format that can be maintained through a back-end interface (without HTML skills)?
E-mail/Comment Forms	Who will receive and respond to user comments? Will comments need to go to different people depending on the topics they address? (For example, will requests for content help be directed to one person and requests for technical assistance be directed to another person?) How will responses be generated? Will we have automated response?
Code and Script	When changes in the coding or scripting of the website are required, who will make them? Are comments included within a page's HTML so that another programmer could easily follow the logic?

Table 4-2
Sample Website Elements and Maintenance Issues

explanation. The suggestions here are meant as starting points to help you in determining which tasks might need to be explored as you identify the maintenance issues of your children's site.

Editing User Input

As noted in chapter 2, allowing children to post their opinions, reviews, or stories on your site is empowering. The editing of their contributions should be limited to simple changes, such as removing inappropriate language or personally identifiable information. To ensure that children can take pride in their material once it is posted, it should not be changed beyond recognition.

Updating Content

Some content that exists on a site when it is launched, such as an events calendar, book reviews, and some games, will need to be changed periodically. The changed material is new to the end user, but it is not new from a development standpoint. Games may seem complicated to create but many can often be recycled with new content. Frequency of updates will differ with the type of content. A hangman-type game can have phrases and categories added to give players "new" ways to play each time they visit. Changing the theme, the pairs to be matched, or the faces on the cards can revitalize a concentration/memory game.

Code and Script

It is a reality that the person who originally develops a site may not be the person who needs to adjust the code later on. This is true whether the code is done by an outside developer or a member of the library staff. There is more than one way to write code to achieve the same result. One developer may use tools such as an HTML editor to create code, and another developer may do everything from scratch. From the beginning, it is imperative that the code be set up with future developers in mind. This will prevent the frustration of having to unravel the secrets of the original developer's code. A simple way to do this is to add comments to the code that explain to the other developers what the code is doing. Such notes are not necessary for every detail—just for the elements that might need interpretation. For example, in figure 4-7, the comments that explain what the code is doing are highlighted.

    The process of identifying individual maintenance issues can be time-consuming. However, the amount of time spent on that task is negligible

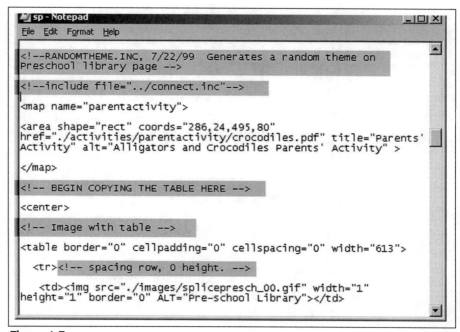

Figure 4-7
Sample Code Explanations for Future Developers

in comparison to the amount of time that will be saved in the future. Examining site elements in terms of maintenance issues lays the groundwork for the creation of a task list and the assignment of responsibilities. Answering the questions outlined in table 4-2 will help you to design a structured maintenance plan for keeping the elements of your site fresh.

IDENTIFYING TASKS AND RESPONSIBILITIES

The process of matching site elements that will require maintenance with the corresponding tasks can also be approached from a flowchart (or if/then) standpoint. Creating a flowchart not only defines tasks and those responsible for them but also identifies tasks that can be streamlined with the creation of an interface.

Consider, for example, how a library might flesh out the issues related to allowing user feedback on its website. As shown in the flowchart in figure 4-8, one key issue would be which method of collecting feedback to use: a simple e-mail link or an input form. If a form is selected, the task is to develop an interface for users to send their comments. This would entail

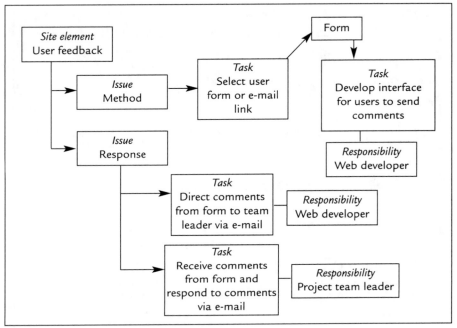

Figure 4-8
Issues Related to Allowing User Feedback on a Website

developing the form and creating a method of sending the form to the staff person responsible for replying.

Although the interface (that is, the input form) is on the user's end, the staff can control its content because it can designate which information, such as an e-mail address, is required. The ability to mandate certain input is especially helpful when children are asking questions or giving opinions. A homework assistance form, for example, might ask children to supply such information as grade level and subject to ensure that the person responding to the questions will understand the amount and kind of information being asked for.

STREAMLINING MAINTENANCE TASKS

Some maintenance tasks require updating or adding the same type of information to a site over and over again. An event calendar, for example, will most likely include information such as the names of programs, dates, times, and descriptions, and will need to be updated frequently. Though the programs differ, the types of information that must be updated remain the same. Book reviews are another example of new content that needs to be added to a site using standard information in a standard format. Both calendar entries and book reviews are good candidates for a maintenance interface. A maintenance interface allows users (public or staff) to add new content to the site using a preset format. When producing a maintenance plan, one key is to identify the tasks that could be best done by creating an interface.

The flowchart in figure 4-9 outlines the maintenance process for a site that will include staff-written reviews of children's books and that will include an interface that enables staff members to add new reviews on a regular basis. The two key tasks are thus the writing of reviews and the creation of an interface for entering reviews into the site. Streamlining maintenance in this case would be advantageous because the same type of information is always added for each book review.

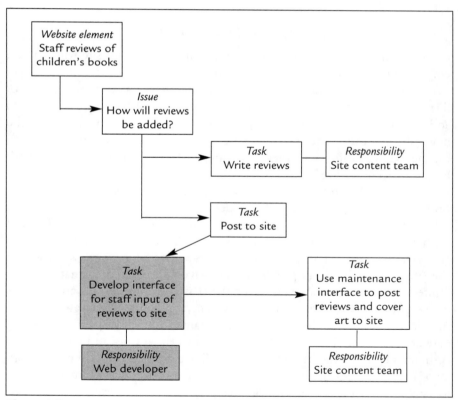

Figure 4-9
Maintenance Process for a Website That Includes Staff-Written Book Reviews

PULLING THE PLAN TOGETHER

The written record of maintenance tasks and the people responsible for performing them will ultimately become the task list part of the maintenance plan. Add any considerations you may have identified about future enhancements and your plan will be complete. Anything you can possibly think of that needs to be done or that might be added to the site should be included in your plan. When thinking of future enhancements, your team need not be psychic. Start by listing things that might have been part of the original concept but needed to be put on hold.

Figure 4-10 contains a sample maintenance plan created for a children's reading center site. The imaginary site features staff-written book reviews, a Name that Book! game, links to author websites, and a book-rating activity. The plan assumes that an interface already exists for the Name that Book! activity.

Building Maintenance Interfaces

Once you have examined what ongoing maintenance your site will require, you can begin to determine where a maintenance interface can help you streamline repetitive tasks. Typically, an interface is a form (or group of forms) connected to an underlying database. Special scripts allow users to add information to the database, which then may automatically post the new information to the site. The entering of information and the posting can be done at different times, allowing staff to double-check their work before it becomes live.

Figures 4-11 and 4-12 show maintenance interfaces developed by the Public Library of Charlotte and Mecklenburg County to streamline areas of two of its websites. The back-end interface in figure 4-11 allows staff to add both new categories and new phrases to the hangman activity on the ImaginOn website. The interface supports a specific activity found within the site and has limited options. It is password protected so that access is limited to staff members who know the password. Categories and phrases contained within the activity may be searched and edited. If a category is to be added, data entry fields for category name, description, and publishing date are required. Once a category is added to the list, it can be selected for editing and phrases can be added to it. Adding a phrase to an existing category involves completing only one field on the form. This interface makes it easy for staff to update the activity by changing or deleting existing items and adding new ones.

READING ROUNDUP MAINTENANCE PLAN

Townville Public Library

Task List

Tasks	Staff Responsible	Frequency
Check that all links are valid; if invalid, change URL or delete link	Content team	Quarterly
Develop interface for inputting new reviews	Web developer	Not applicable
Write new reviews and post to site using reviews interface	Content team	5 new reviews per month
Add new phrases to Name that Book! game using existing game interface	Content team	Monthly
Respond to feedback	Site team leader	Daily
Change books listed for rating activity Create list of 52 or so activities that can randomly change weekly	Content team	Within 30 days

Timeline for Enhancements

Tasks	Frequency
Update features based on user feedback	Review every 2 months
Add new author links	Monthly
Explore new subjects for links	3 months
Explore new features to enhance reviews	6 months
Create new game	9 months
Add children's book reviews	1 year

Figure 4-10
Sample Website Maintenance Plan

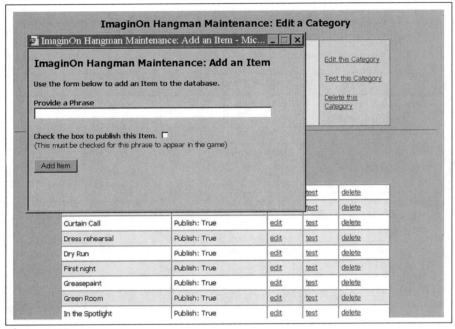

Figure 4-11
ImaginOn Hangman Maintenance Interface (http://www.imaginon.org), Public Library of Charlotte and Mecklenburg County, Charlotte, North Carolina

The maintenance interface for the BookHive website, shown in figure 4-12, enables staff to perform seven different maintenance tasks for the site. Each task has its own form, with all tasks always accessible from the top of the page. Additional forms may be added to the interface as new features that contain an ongoing maintenance component are developed. The screen capture shows the top of the input form for adding a book review. Some field descriptors (such as Author, Title, Publisher, and Pub Date) are boldfaced, which indicates that they are required.

Updating the Site

Once a maintenance plan is drafted and the maintenance interfaces are created, all that remains to be done is the follow-through. The site is now live, but the work has just begun. It is important for the site team to continue

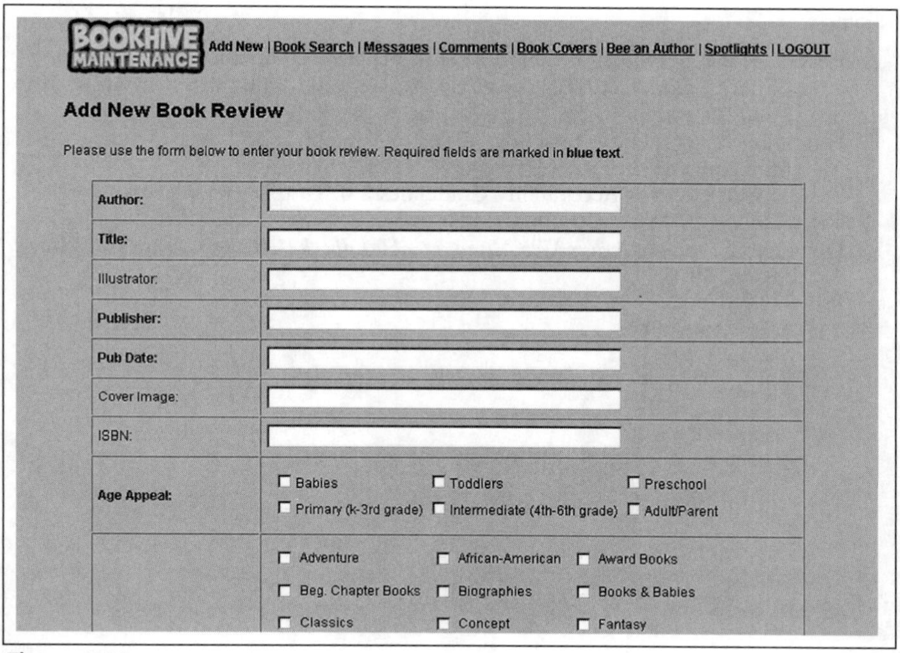

Figure 4-12
BookHive Maintenance Interface (http://www.bookhive.org), Public Library of
Charlotte and Mecklenburg County, Charlotte, North Carolina

to meet regularly to apprise each other of progress on assigned tasks and to deal with new ideas and issues. The schedule laid out in the maintenance plan should be followed or adjusted as needed. It is crucial that maintenance tasks be completed in a timely manner, and holding meetings that allow team members to report to each other on a *regular basis* can help everyone stay on track.

The key to a successful maintenance plan is preparation, streamlined updates, and follow-through. Create your plan, make or find the tools to keep maintenance simple, and stick to the schedule. Our library has found that the success of our websites is due in part to our monthly team meetings, which enable us to go over timelines, exchange progress reports, and stay on task. The importance of developing and following through on such invisible background work should never be underestimated, for it ensures that a site will be well run.

NOTES

1. Federal Trade Commission, "New Rule to Protect Children's Online Privacy Takes Effect April 21, 2000," press release, April 20, 2000, http://www.ftc.gov/opa/2000/04/coppal.htm (accessed March 15, 2004).
2. Watchfire, "Accessibility: Enabling Access to Your Business," http://www.watchfire.com/resources/bobby-overview.pdf.
3. W3C, "Web Content Accessibility Guidelines 2.0," http://www.w3c.org/TR/2004/WD-WCA 920-20040311.
4. Dowling, Thomas, *Library Web Manager's Handbook* (Chicago: American Library Association, 2003).
5. Ibid.

CHAPTER 5

Building a Team

The development of engaging and interactive websites for children can be complex. Fast-moving technology and new methodologies can complicate the picture just as much as changes in user needs and expectations. Because of these shifting factors, finding a comfortable development approach is important. With the advent of the Internet, many information technology developers have reshaped their methodologies from a traditional top-down model to a collaborative model that takes better advantage of the collective expertise that all team members bring to the table. In a collaborative approach, project team members share the responsibility of ensuring their project's completion. Management of the project is assumed not only by the project manager but by all members of the project team, who work together toward a shared vision and a common goal. This approach places an emphasis on shared responsibilities and accentuates the notion that all team members' ideas are equally worthy and that every person's contribution is valuable. In a collaborative team process, not only does the project itself benefit from a collective perspective, but individual team members benefit as well. Individual team members[1]

Experience greater productivity and produce higher quality work

Feel empowered and are easily motivated to share their ideas and accept feedback from others

Share in the decision-making process, which helps to build team unity in reaching a common goal

Overall, a collaborative model benefits both the final outcome of a project and the personal objectives of the team members, and it provides the users of children's web services with a higher quality product. Given the collaborative approach's many benefits, it is easy to see why so many organizations have embraced it.

Building a team atmosphere will nourish your development process and empower project team members to succeed. Although it is important to have individuals with strong skill sets and imaginative minds on your team, it is equally important that they all work well together. To create an atmosphere of collaboration and shared responsibilities, team members should[2]

Share a common goal or vision for the project

Understand how each person's roles and responsibilities contribute to the success of the project

Communicate constantly about their project tasks and be willing to keep their minds and ears open to all suggestions

Appreciate diversity and remember that each team member brings something unique to the development process

Be willing to balance the effectiveness and focus of team (the internal group dynamics and relationships) with the quality of the services and products under development—that is, avoid compromising the product just to accommodate individual team members' tastes or wishes

Collaborative teams work best when they are guided by leaders who lead by example, who are open to any and all suggestions, and who are able to consistently communicate that the success of the project lies within the shared achievement of its team. This approach requires not only strong team members but also a team leader who can simultaneously recognize individual members' contributions and emphasize the accomplishments of the team. No web development project can succeed without the collective skills of many different individuals. Therefore it is important to seek out talent and select team members wisely.

ASSEMBLING A PROJECT TEAM

Creating an innovative site for children takes more than great ideas and a collaborative team approach; you also need strong team members to bring the ideas to life. Therefore, selecting the right team members for your project is critical. One of the first steps in the selection process is to identify the skill sets of the team members you will need to get the project going. With most web development projects, the team members typically fall into one of three categories:

1. Content creators (or content experts): the team members who provide the substance for the site
2. Web developers: programmers or web designers who make the content accessible through the Web
3. Advisers: staff whose knowledge and experience assist in guiding the development of the project

The team leader, who sets the stage for the collaborative team, ideally fits into the picture somewhere between the three, having not only the expertise to complete key tasks for the project but also the knowledge to lead the project to completion. In addition, a team leader must have excellent communication skills to keep everyone informed and on the same track.

Ideally a project team should have no more than six or seven members. In general, the more members you have beyond that number, the less productive the development team is likely to be. When establishing your team, make sure that all members are fully aware of their roles, their responsibilities, and the amount of time that will be required of them. Spelling out such information at the very beginning is critical to getting your project off on the right foot.

The Team Leader

Every project needs at least one individual who will guide the team through the development process. In many organizations that person is called a project manager. However, in a collaborative team process, where many of the management responsibilities are shared and the boundaries of the project may be ambiguous, the title of team leader seems to be a much better fit. The differences between the two titles are more than simple semantics.[3]

- A manager takes care of where you are; a leader takes you to a new place—where you want to be.
- A manager deals with complexity; a leader deals with uncertainty.
- A manager is concerned with doing things right; a leader is concerned with doing the right things.
- A manager's critical concern is efficiency; a leader focuses on effectiveness.

The role of the team leader in the web development process is to guide the project team in tackling the unknown through such activities as developing the project plan, defining the project's architecture, orchestrating the project's development, and documenting the project's achievements (or failures). Like the head chef of a fine restaurant, the project leader must bring together all the key players to create a pièce de résistance.

Although the primary responsibilities of a project team leader involve coordinating individual team members' tasks and efforts, the leader should also have some skills to contribute to the creation of content. Finding the right individual (or individuals) to lead a team can sometimes be a difficult task, especially if members of your library supervisory staff are already overburdened. Staff members who work with the public every day but who do not have supervisory responsibility for the library's day-to-day operations often make the best team leaders because they have more energy and time to devote to a project. A project leader who does not feel pulled in too many directions and who comes from within the ranks of your nonsupervisory staff will enhance the team's esprit de corps and emphasize the collaborative nature of the project.

Content Creators

The development of a website for children cannot move forward without content creators—staff members who will create and write the real substance for the project. Some people like to refer to these team members as content experts, and indeed they are. However, we like to refer to them as content creators, because that term more accurately describes the active role they play in the project. Content creators have the responsibility of creating the subject matter and materials that will be available to and used by children on the site. This includes writing copy, outlining design details, storyboarding layouts, and providing first-level testing and feedback to guide developers in creating the desired end product. If your website design includes a maintenance interface or data entry forms that will allow team members to publish content directly on the site, the responsibility of populating the site with information lies with the content creators as well.

It is important to select content specialists carefully. First make sure that any staff member you add to the team has the commitment and time to participate. It is also crucial to secure the approval and support of each potential team member's supervisors. Web development projects often fall behind due to delays in producing and delivering content, which in turn pushes back web design and development. It is easy for content creators to fall behind if all staff members, and especially the creators' supervisors, do not share the priorities of the project. If your content creators' time is adequately freed to develop material for the site and if they have their management's support, your project should proceed on schedule.

When selecting individuals to join your team as content creators, look for staff members who are highly creative and imaginative and have sharp, concise writing skills. It is a well-known fact that, in general, people do not read websites, they scan them. In fact, a study done in the late 1990s found that only 16 percent of users surveyed actually read web pages, whereas 79 percent quickly scanned them for key words.[4] That finding is significant enough to influence your choice of content creators, especially if your project involves large amounts of material or information. In developing the Hands on Crafts site (http://www.handsoncrafts.org), we experienced the importance of this firsthand. Halfway through the project's development we discovered that the majority of our written content was far too lengthy to fit properly within the screen and that the amount of detail was too overwhelming for the average fourth-grader to absorb. Fortunately for us, our design firm was able to guide us through the process of editing the content down to a comprehensible level and a manageable size. But without their knowledge and help, the outcome would have been much different from the highly engaging and educational website about North Carolina crafts that we ultimately produced. In content creators, solid writing and communication skills are almost as important as content knowledge itself.

Advisers

Advisers play an important part in the development of any web project by providing the knowledge and experience that will help get the project off the ground. They are especially valuable during the early planning and late testing phases of a project. However, the greatest mistake that many website planners make is to load their team with too many advisers and not enough developers or content creators. Just as too many cooks can spoil the broth, too many advisers can stifle the website-development process.

When selecting advisers for your project team, look for individuals within your library system who have had experience with similar types of innovative projects and who are respected by key members of your staff. It never hurts to have someone on your team who can pull a few strings if your project resources become stretched too thin. Advisers can also assist the team in coming up with creative solutions to difficult work situations, which may help make the project go much smoother. It never hurts to have a good adviser or two on your project team—just avoid the temptation to have too many.

Web Developers

Web developers bring all the ingredients of a great website together. With a little luck and a lot of skill, the outcome of their magic is an attractive website that keeps users enticed, provides valuable content and information, and is quick and easy to use. Finding the right web developer or web design firm to work with on your children's website is as important as making sure you have highly imaginative content creators. And depending upon the needs of your project, you may need the services of two different types of web developers.

DESIGNERS

Designers, also known as graphic artists, help to make your new children's web service exciting for users. Finding the right look for your website is almost as vital as ensuring that your site meets the service goals you have set. If the site does not appeal to children, then all the time and effort that was put into its development will be wasted. If you do not already have a web designer on your staff, you can look outside your library. Web development companies can often provide skillful designers and programmers to fit your project's needs. Occasionally, you might be lucky enough to find an individual who excels in both areas, but that is very rare.

When screening designers, do not be afraid to ask for samples of their work. You might even ask final candidates to mock up a simple design using some of your project's specifications. This will assist you in determining if a contender's design approach and artistic style are what you seek. Our experience has shown that if a designer is truly interested in working on your project, he or she will be willing to put in some extra effort to get the contract. Even after you have selected a designer or a design firm, you need not feel obligated to accept the first design that is presented. Keep in mind that you are paying for the designer's services and that you know what will work best in reaching out to children. A good designer should accept and act on your comments and criticisms, and should also involve other members of the project team in the design process. A good web developer recognizes that it takes more than a good designer to develop a great web service for children—it takes a whole team of creative minds.

PROGRAMMERS

Ensuring that your site is appealing and interesting to young users is indeed important, but you also want to make sure that the code behind the site's engaging design and flashy images is solid and conforms to usability standards and W3C protocols and specifications. This can be accomplished by having a strong web programmer on your team.

A good programmer makes your site efficient and usable with code and scripts that work behind the scenes to ensure your site is easily accessible to all users. Writing and verifying good code is not the glamorous part of web development, but it is fundamental to the usability of your site and requires more than simple HTML knowledge.

In the last few years, as websites have become more sophisticated, web developers have come to need far more than simple markup language skills. Good web developers should also be proficient in some type of scripting language, such as PERL, ASP, or Java, and know how to interface with databases, such as SQL or Access. With such skills, most web developers can build sites that not only work well but also are efficient and effective across many web platforms. If you are lucky enough, you may already have a skilled web developer on your staff. If not, you will need to consider hiring an outside developer.

OUTSIDE DEVELOPERS

It would be wonderful if you could find all the people you need to develop your new children's web service among your library staff. However, that may not be possible, especially if you do not have a dedicated web developer or designer on your payroll. If your staff does not already have all the needed skills, you will probably want to seek the assistance of an outside developer or a web development firm. Working with an outside developer can provide many benefits as well as a few possible drawbacks. The trick is to find a developer or design firm that you feel comfortable working with and that will provide the most advantages.

Benefits

The obvious reason for hiring an outside developer is to obtain the technical (programming, scripting, XML) or graphical expertise you need to develop your new children's web service, but there are other considerations as well. One of the greatest benefits of working with someone outside your staff is that the resulting customer-vendor relationship will assist you in directing the development of the project. For example, working with an outside developer frees you to provide criticism and suggestions without having to worry about stepping on another staff member's toes.

In addition, an outside developer can look at your project from a fresh perspective, offering you the viewpoint of a potential user without preconceptions about what your new web service should (or should not) offer. Of course, a developer's lack of familiarity with your project may be a drawback as well, but only a minor one. Our experience suggests that having a fresh perspective can be a great help in identifying potential design and functionality problems that might not be obvious to people who have worked in the same organization for a long time. Such a situation arose as we were redesigning our library's information site.

For several weeks a cross-section of our staff diligently worked on identifying and categorizing all the informational elements we wanted our library's site to contain (books, programs, and so forth). To no one's great surprise, information about the library's books, CD and movie collections, audiotape books, and the like rose to the top of the list. The team struggled to come up with a good category name to group these elements under and finally settled on "collections" because it best described all the materials that our library provided. However, it was not until we hired a new developer that we saw the folly in our choice. To him, the word "collections" immediately brought to mind creditors telephoning people and harassing them to pay overdue bills. For him, that term on a library site immediately had a negative connotation because he assumed it identified where information on overdue fines and other library fees could be found. Of course, that was certainly not what we had intended, but we were too close to the source of the term—ourselves—to be able to identify it as a potential problem. His outside perspective helped us to see the situation in a new light and find a remedy.

Drawbacks

As already mentioned, there are possible drawbacks to collaborating with a developer who is not familiar with the inner workings of your library. The greatest potential problem is that the developer you have chosen may not accord your project the same importance or urgency that you do. If the developer has several other projects in progress or is committed to performing ongoing maintenance and updates for other clients, your project might suffer.

During your interview and selection process, be sure to ask all candidates how many and what kinds of web projects they typically work on simultaneously and how many sites they are under contract to maintain. If a candidate seems very busy, ask how your project will fit into the current project load and what the person plans to do to ensure that your project will get the attention it needs. Your goal is to find someone who has the expertise and experience you desire, who understands your project needs and objectives, and who views your project the same way you do, as top priority. Achieving this goal can be easier if you use a request for proposal (RFP) process.

Request for Proposal

According to F. John Reh, "Probably the biggest source of confusion and cause for problems between nonprofits and Internet development companies is a poorly written Request for Proposal (RFP)."[5] An RFP is a written document that aids you in surveying potential web developers and soliciting competitive bids for the development of your project. Of paramount importance to your RFP is your project plan (see chapter 6), which will communicate the scope of your project and background information about your organization to candidates for your web development job.

The project plan and RFP will help you clarify your thinking about your website. Many libraries have only a fuzzy vision of their desired website and depend too heavily on an outside web developer to tell them what they can do. As a result, both parties may become frustrated—the web developer because he or she cannot get a clear picture of what the client wants and the library because the project does not seem to be developing in the direction that was originally envisioned. Creating an RFP can assist in eliminating some of the confusion.

The goals of an RFP are to attract well-designed and reasonable proposals from developers, to establish a comfortable working relationship between your library and the web developer you ultimately choose, and to clarify the expectations of both parties. A sample RFP is presented in the appendix.

FORMALIZING THE PROCESS

Once you have created a project plan, you are nearly halfway through the RFP-creation process because that plan will help you share key information about your project with the web developer or design firm you hope to work with. Three additional items you may want to include in your RFP document are

1. A brief description of your library and its overall mission for children, including information about similar projects your library may

have produced so that potential developers will better understand your staff's preferences and experience.

2. A time frame for completing the project. This will automatically weed out some developers who already have other projects slated for the same time frame.

3. A description of the resources you intend to devote to the project. Knowing how many members of your staff will be working on the project and what roles they will play will help developers gauge the scope of their involvement and the amount of help you will need.

The next step is to seek out a handful of web developers or companies that you feel might be interested in your project. To develop this list, ask the advice of similar organizations in your area. Find out who has done web development work for them, whom they would recommend, and whom they would advise you to avoid. If your list is too short, you might want to think about posting an ad in your local newspaper or on a local web development bulletin board. Many larger communities have web developer groups that help their members to keep up with emerging web trends and to network with others in the field. If you decide to use a newspaper ad, your copy should be short and to the point. For example:

> Townsville Public Library seeks web developer to help build children's website that will automate summer reading program, including online registration, information about library programs, and interactive activities (Flash). Interested development companies or individuals should e-mail Ida B. Manager at Imanager@library.org before 10/15 for details.

Once you have compiled a list of prospects, you can send them your formal RFP document along with a description of exactly what information you expect the proposals to contain. This will allow you to more easily evaluate proposals using an apples-to-apples comparison. For example, your cover letter might outline the following expectations:

> **Proposals should contain the following sections:**
>
> Summary of your development approach to this project
>
> An estimated timeline for completing the project, with milestones and review processes clearly identified
>
> Your estimated cost for the project, broken down into components, plus details of payment
>
> Background information about yourself or your company

> Professional qualifications and samples of work, including
>   relevant URLs
> References: names and contact information of a minimum
>   of three previous clients who are familiar with your work

Depending on the nature of your project, you may want to request other information, but you can save many of your questions for the screening interviews you will have with your final few candidates.

Your RFP should generate several proposals from qualified web developers. You can then select two or three of the best proposals and invite the individuals or web development firms to interview with members of your project team. Be sure to ask candidates to come prepared to discuss their ideas and proposals, and tell them how to contact you if they have questions about the process. Don't be surprised if some developers come prepared to show you far more than you asked for. Some may even develop prototypes for your project that can be helpful in assessing the capabilities and skills they can bring to a project. Often, it is the most eager and enthusiastic developer who will best fit your project's needs and will deliver a more innovative children's website than you ever imagined.

The RFP process is important because finding the right developer is critical to the successful completion of your project. No matter how strong the rest of your project team may be, if you select a developer who does not share your vision and enthusiasm for the project, the final results are bound to be disappointing both to you and to your target audience. Rest assured that even in the best development relationships, all participants make mistakes. Delivery dates will slip, your project team will be delayed in supplying content, and unanticipated problems will arise. The solution is to select a web developer who is as willing to forgive your mistakes as you are to forgive his or hers. Therefore, finding a compatible web developer is fundamental to the overall success of the project.

DEVELOPING EFFECTIVE TEAMS

Once you have selected all the members of your project team, the next step is to lay the groundwork that will enable the team to function effectively. It takes more than the right individuals to put together an outstanding children's website—it takes a team with clearly established and shared expectations, defined roles and responsibilities, and strong communication skills. Starting the project with a clear set of plans for communication, follow-up, and contingencies will help the team to coalesce and function effectively.

Communication Plan. Determine the best method for keeping every-one informed about the project's progress (including team members, administrators, and anyone else who needs to be kept in the know). Specify methods of delivery and project documentation. How often will the team meet? What is the best method of sharing updates?

Follow-up Plan. Determine the best way of keeping team members apprised of the project deadlines and milestones. Establish ways to document team members' responsibilities and assignments and the project's status.

Contingency Plan. Recognize that 99 percent of all projects do not proceed as originally anticipated. Deadlines will slip, simple tasks will balloon, and unexpected complications will arise. These are all normal occurrences and will happen despite the best-laid plans. Contingency plans identify and address potential problems so that everyone will be prepared to deal with them when they emerge. Keep your options open and recognize that everything will not go according to plan.

Finding and bringing together the right people to create an effective web development team can be challenging. However, managing a web development project is a bit easier if you keep in mind Pareto's Principle, or the 80-20 rule:

80 percent of your project will consume only 20 percent of your time, but the last 20 percent of the project will take 80 percent of your time.[6]

The key to managing your project is to keep the team focused on making progress on the more difficult activities that will consume the greatest amount of their time. It is tempting to tend to the 80 percent of the project that is uncomplicated or familiar, but the most effective teams concentrate on the 20 percent that is difficult or unfamiliar. Tackle the demanding activities first if you want to keep the development and implementation of your children's web service on target.

In preparing this chapter, we found numerous books offering dozens of approaches to the management of web development projects. The reason there are so many approaches is that almost everyone is still trying to figure it out! In truth, there is no simple, tried-and-true method of managing a successful web project. Just as the web environment itself is constantly changing, there is always a new way to manage a project or enhance group dynamics within a project team. But no matter what type of project is involved, several key characteristics make effective project teams stand out. In his book *Project Zen*, Jack Ricchiuto describes the zen of highly effective project teams as follows:[7]

> Effective project teams are known for their ability to live and work in harmony with reality—*whatever it is.*
>
> They are not easily distracted or discouraged by change or uncertainty.
>
> They do not fight with projects; they do not resist the challenges and opportunities that projects present.
>
> They approach projects with a sense of composure. Seeing things as they are, they work in harmony with reality as it is.

If you follow this logic, then the real trick to managing a project is to find the middle ground for your project and your team that will facilitate anticipating and dealing with the unexpected. Ultimately your project's success does not depend on how well you have defined your project plan, or on how skilled your team members are, or even on how many resources you have at your disposal. All those elements do help, but the true key to success is your team's ability to handle, create, and deal with change. Recognizing that change lies at the core of successful project management is the first step toward finding your project's harmony.

NOTES

1. Stewart L. Stokes Jr., "Building Effective Project Teams," *Information Systems Management 7*, no. 3 (Summer 1990): 38.
2. United States Office of Personnel Management, "Building a Collaborative Team Environment," *Work Performance Newsletter,* August 1997, http://www.opm .gov/perform/articles/072.htm (accessed July 28, 2003).
3. James Colvard, "Managers vs. Leaders," *Government Executive Magazine,* July 7, 2003, http://www.govexec.com/dailyfed/0703/070703ff.htm (accessed January 19, 2004).
4. Jakob Nielsen, "How Users Read on the Web," useit.com, October 1, 1997, http://www.useit.com/alertbox/9710a.html (accessed July 30, 2003).
5. F. John Reh, "Pareto's Principle—The 80-20 Rule," http://management .about.com/library/weekly/aa081202.htm (accessed July 14, 2003).
6. Bruce Morris, "How to Write a Request for Proposal for a Web Project," http://www.webdevelopersjournal.com/columns/writerfp.html (accessed July 12, 2003).
7. Jack Ricchiuto, "Project Zen Intro," DesigningLife.com, http://www .designing-life.com/ProjectZenIntro.htm (accessed January 19, 2004)

CHAPTER 6

Planning and Organization

**RECIPE FOR A GREAT
CHILDREN'S WEBSITE**

Ingredients:

1 project team full of imagination

1 large helping of creativity

1 dash of opportunity

A whole lot of ingenuity

Mix all four ingredients together and bake in web development oven. Add marketing garnishes and serve.

It takes more than a good idea to develop a new Internet service for children. It takes time, resources, talent, and, most importantly, a well-defined idea. You might think of the process as the creation of a great recipe. The best chefs in the world often try out new recipes in test kitchens, bringing in taste experts, other cooks, and even people off the street to sample their new creations. As a really great recipe is developed, the ingredients may be altered and modified many times based on input from a variety of people. Only when the recipe is perfected is it written down for others to duplicate and enjoy. Although recipes for great websites are seldom duplicated in exactly the same way, the process of developing and refining the recipe, or the idea, is very similar.

REFINING A GOOD IDEA

To refine an idea for a new children's web service, begin by establishing an overall goal for your project. Then gather suggestions from your project team, colleagues, and intended users (children and their parents) about how best to achieve that goal. Information technology organizations often call this phase of a project concept development.

In writing this chapter of the book, we were constantly reminded about a concept that we were challenged with by a library director a few years ago—to develop a digital library for children. His idea was very philosophical and undeveloped, but it got us started on developing an idea for children's web service that eventually became StoryPlace (http://www.story place.org). The library director did give us two basic directives that assisted us in the development process: that the site should be bilingual (in Spanish and English) and that we should start by reaching our youngest users—preschool-age children. Thus we had at least a few of the ingredients we would need to begin developing our project's recipe. Arriving at the other necessary elements required a lot of input from our customers and our project team.

Two of the most common methods of seeking input from others when refining a website concept are brainstorming sessions and focus groups. In our experience, both methods work well. With brainstorming sessions, you get not only great ideas that help you define the core service you want to develop but also a flurry of nice-to-have ideas that you can possibly add as future enhancements to your site.

Focus groups allow you to take your preliminary concept directly to the potential users of your site. Through informal discussions and open-ended questions you can gather useful information about what users would like to see in a new children's library Internet service. There is an established methodology for conducting focus groups, complete with ground rules, facilitator guidelines, and question-formulation rules that help to stimulate lively input from users. That methodology is too complex to go into in this book, but it is sufficient to note that conducting focus group sessions with members of your intended audience will yield valuable information you can use in refining the concept for your new children's website.

Let the Brainstorming Begin

Brainstorming is a creative process that allows for the free flow of ideas. It is designed to help people break out of their usual thinking patterns and find new ways of looking at things. In group brainstorming sessions, all participants are encouraged to contribute freely so that lots of different ideas (both good and bad) are generated. Criticism or analysis of ideas has no place in this creative process. The goal of brainstorming is to generate new ideas, not to develop them. Any and all ideas that are generated should be evaluated only by the project team after the brainstorming session has finished.

The participants in a brainstorming session should come from as many different backgrounds as possible. Such diversity brings a broad range of experience to the session and helps to generate lots of creative ideas. Adhering to the following guidelines will make your group brainstorming as productive as possible:[1]

> Share the goal or mission of your project. Stating the goal or mission very broadly will encourage the generation of ideas.
>
> Keep participants focused on the purpose of the meeting.
>
> Ensure that no one criticizes or evaluates ideas during the session. Judgmental comments stifle creativity and thwart the free flow of ideas.
>
> Encourage an enthusiastic, uncritical attitude among participants. Gather ideas from everyone, including the quietest members of the group. Do not allow one person to monopolize the conversation.
>
> Encourage group members to feed off each other's ideas to develop new ideas.
>
> Appoint one person to jot down all the ideas on a flipchart or whiteboard so that everyone can see them.
>
> Most importantly, let people have fun! Encourage them to come up with as many wildly impractical ideas as possible. Sometimes what at first sounds like the craziest idea is both desirable and obtainable.

Once the brainstorming session is completed, have your project team evaluate all suggestions. With luck you may come up with several concrete ideas that can be developed into your website.

Developing a Project Plan

A project plan is a formal document that outlines all the components you will need to make your project a success. Think of it as the road map that will guide you through the development process and past any stumbling blocks you may encounter along the way. Your project plan should contain as much specific information as possible, such as:

Background: How did this project come about?

Mission: What is the overall purpose of your site?

Objectives: How do you want users to benefit from your website?

Audience: Whom do you want to benefit most from your website? What are the interests, needs, and skill levels of that group? What groups will be the site's secondary audiences?

Requirements: What must the site do for users and what would it be nice to have? What functions must users be able to perform? (Keep in mind that nice-to-have elements can always be added later.)

Implementation Plan: How do you plan to roll out the project? Are there any target dates that must be met, such as the starting date of a summer reading program or the first day of the school year?

Evaluation: How do you plan to measure the success of your project?

Key Players: Who are your sponsors, stakeholders, and project team members?

Not every project plan needs to include all of the preceding information. However, if you lack a well-defined mission statement, a clear set of objectives, and an identified target audience, it is unlikely that your project will ever be completed. If you do not have a clear vision of how you want children (and other audiences) to benefit from your new service, your development efforts and those of the people who have agreed to assist you will be lost.

A sample project plan is presented in figure 6-1. It is a scaled-down version of the actual project plan that was created for the development of the Public Library of Charlotte and Mecklenburg County's StoryPlace website. If you compare the condensed project plan with the actual site, you will see that virtually all the requirements outlined in the initial plan were met. The one requirement that was eventually excluded from the final version of the site was the sing-along activity. When the project team started to develop content for sing-along activities, they ran into copyright issues and decided to provide parent's activity sheets instead. The project plan helped keep everyone on target and enabled us to complete and roll out the site, which offered four themes, in ten months.

CHILDREN'S DIGITAL LIBRARY PROJECT PLAN
Public Library of Charlotte and Mecklenburg County

Mission	To use the interactive nature of the Internet to deliver children and their caregivers enhanced online activities (in both English and Spanish) that mirror the types of reading-enrichment activities children receive when they attend a library story hour.
Objectives	To provide children with a theme-based online experience that stimulates reading, the love of books, and language development. To provide parents and caregivers with a safe, commercial-free website that they can direct children to. To provide an online mechanism for recommending good reading books for children. To provide a new online service for children that supports the Spanish-speaking population as well as those wanting to learn Spanish or English. To create a new model for children's library services on the Web.
Audience	The primary audience for this site will be preschool-age children (five years of age and under). Secondary audiences are parents, caregivers, older children, ESL students, Spanish-language students, other libraries, or anyone interested in the reading development of children.

Requirements	The website design should incorporate the following requirements:
	
	A different learning concept/theme that is highlighted daily or set on a rotating schedule. Each theme should contain:
	
	    Online story
	    Online activity
	    Take-home activity
	    Sing-along activity
	    Suggested reading list
	
	Parents and children should have access to the whole list of concepts so they can listen to other stories and do other activities at their will

Website design should be very colorful and engaging to children and include lots of animation.

Website should be available in multiple languages. We could start with English and Spanish and possibly add more languages later.

Website design should contain lots of audio as well as visual stimulation.

Website design should allow for future expansion to include stories and activities for older children.

Figure 6-1
Sample Project Plan for a Children's Website

An Approach to Success

Another tool that can be useful during your project's development is an approach-to-success document. This tool helps you define the desired effects and outcomes of your new children's web service. It can be especially helpful if you find yourself in the position of seeking administrative or upper-management support for the project. By documenting what you expect your new children's service to achieve, you also begin to establish the parameters that can be used to measure its success.

In developing an approach-to-success document, ask yourself the following questions:

What goals of your library's mission statement relate to the objectives of your new children's web service?

How will your new children's web service support the library's mission and goals?

How will children (and adults) use the new service to reach the site's objectives?

How will you measure the project's success?

Although an approach-to-success document covers some of the same basic elements (such as mission and goals) as a project plan, the two are written for very different audiences. A project plan is written mostly for the members of the project team, who will be doing the actual development work. It outlines specific objectives and requirements as they relate to the overall goals of the *project*. An approach-to-success document outlines the project's goals and objectives as they relate to the overall mission of the *library*. It is not always necessary to create such a document. However, if you find yourself in the position of having to justify funding or solicit support for the project, this type of document can prove useful.

Figure 6-2 presents a sample approach-to-success document for the Public Library of Charlotte and Mecklenburg County's Train Your Brain summer reading project. In 2003, the library pioneered a new online service for teens that used the Internet to completely automate the logistics, tracking, and management of its teen summer reading program. To address staff concerns and to establish a model for the site's development, the project leader came up with the document in figure 6-2.[2]

TRAIN YOUR BRAIN 2003
Approach to Success
http://www.plcmc.org/tyb

Library mission: summer reading

To support and encourage teens to read for fun, learn something new, and make meaningful connections all summer long

Train Your Brain supports this by

Offering an online reading program that encourages teens (rising sixth- to twelfth-graders) to read for pleasure

Supporting teens' reading success by offering a service that allows them to track their reading, journal, and share ideas about what they have read through a personalized online reading log and link

Offering quality incentives to participants for registering and for reading

Encouraging teens to get involved and make connections in their communities by offering engaging programs at all library locations

Offering a constant level of interaction and personalized attention to teens through one-on-one communication in branches and through online conversations that address the inquiries of teens

Teens respond by

Creating personalized reading profiles and reading records

Visiting the TYB website regularly throughout the summer to update personal information and read updates

Entering weekly polls offered on the website

Using the library coupons offered to participants at sign-up, 20 hours, and 40 hours

Offering their opinions and comments on various teen-related subjects through the site

Attending TYB programs at branch libraries

Offering information concerning how TYB affected their lives through follow-up correspondence, an end-of-summer survey, and feedback forms

Because of Train Your Brain teen participants will

Be connected to helpful and supportive adults

Read more

Have productive interactions with other teens

Learn new information and useful skills

The library will measure this by

Documenting participants' responses throughout the program

Administering an evaluative survey to all participants at the end of the program

Tracking participants' registrations and completion levels (10, 20, 30, and 40 hours)

Tracking the number of online inquiries from teens and the number of teens attending branch programs

Figure 6-2
Sample Approach-to-Success Document

STORYBOARDING

Once your project plan has been finalized, you can begin developing meaningful and useful content, which is by far the most important element of any successful website. To work effectively with website developers, you need to be able to share your vision of how the site's content will be used. Storyboarding, a technique borrowed from the film industry, not only aids web developers in designing the site you envision but also assists your project team members in visualizing how information will be organized and presented on the site.

Storyboarding is the process of organizing on paper your ideas for a website. It helps you tell the story of how your site will be defined structurally and what the pages will look like. Storyboarding is a critical part of the content-development phase because it allows everyone to see the big picture of the project before beginning any of the actual web design or web development. Some people may refer to storyboards as flowcharts, organizational charts, or even screen views because they all can be components of a fully developed storyboard. But whatever you decide to call it, be sure to take advantage of this valuable tool.

The process of storyboarding a website involves three tasks:

1. Charting the organizational structure of the site
2. Outlining the directory structure and naming conventions for the site
3. Sketching the design of the individual pages

When all three tasks are completed, you will have finished the content-development phase of your project and will be ready to begin the design phase.

Diagramming the Site's Structure

Diagramming on paper the physical organization of your website is the best way to see and to communicate the site's overall structure. The process of diagramming a site's structure helps all members of the project team identify how large the site will be and what relationships need to be established between the site's various information elements (or pages). There are two different approaches to diagramming a site's structure, each of which is equally valuable. An organizational chart approach works best for very large website projects, when a site will be broken down into several different sections or components. This approach helps viewers see the hierarchical structure of a site by organizing and grouping the informational sections that will be accessible from the home page. Since each section of a site is likely to have multiple pages, or levels, the structural diagram can quickly become unruly if you try to document all of the pages' interrelationships on one piece of paper. In such a case, it may be desirable to break the site into manageable sections and diagram each one separately. The organizational chart that was created for the development of the Public Library of Charlotte and Mecklenburg County's StoryPlace website is shown in figure 6-3.

In contrast, a flowchart approach works well for much smaller sites that contain only a few pages or sections. With a flowchart approach, the organization of a site is defined by the relationships between the sections and pages rather than by the hierarchy of information. The flowchart is a visual representation of the sequence that users will follow as they move around

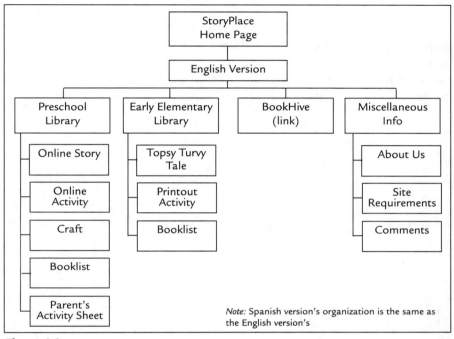

Figure 6-3
Organizational Chart for the Development of the StoryPlace Website

the website. Figure 6-4 presents the flowchart created for the development of Public Library of Charlotte and Mecklenburg County's 2003 summer reading website, Mission READ (http://www.plcmc.org/missionread).

A comparison of figures 6-3 and 6-4 illustrates how the two approaches differ. The organizational chart method emphasizes the hierarchical structure of a site, whereas the flowchart method highlights the relationships between a site's pages. Creating a detailed flowchart for each section can be especially valuable if many complex processes occur within your site. The two approaches have equal merit, and in some cases you may want to use both, especially if your site is going to be large. Since both tools essentially create a working map of your website, the results are not set in stone. In fact, as you begin to create the content and design the pages of your site, you will probably make several modifications to your original layout. Design changes are normal in any web-development project.

The choice of approach—organizational chart, flowchart, or a combination of both—is up to you. The important thing is not to overlook this step in the development process. Diagramming the structure of your website not only will assist team members in getting a handle on the size and scope of your project but will also provide a checklist that you can use to record completed sections of the site as you work through its development.

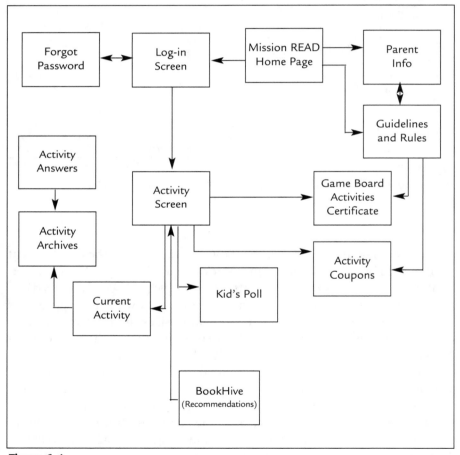

Figure 6-4
Flowchart for the Development of the Mission READ Website

Directory and Naming Conventions

Another important step in creating a storyboard for your children's website is to determine the directory structure and naming conventions that your site will use. Names that describe the information that will be found on the pages seem to work best and allow developers to build the site around a naming structure that will be easy for everyone to follow. For instance, the pages in a summer reading site for kids might be named as follows:

Home

Registration input screen

Registration review screen

Registration confirmation screen

Game card (recording log)

Coloring pages

Guidelines and rules

Reading recommendations

In outlining the pages that the site will contain, you can see that pages involving the registration function can be grouped together. Given this, you might want to combine those pages in their own directory and adopt meaningful names for your files as follows:

Home	/home.htm
Registration input screen	/registration/rg_input.asp
Registration review screen	/registration/rg_review.asp
Registration confirmation screen	/registration/rg_confirm.asp
Game card (recording log)	/gamecard.htm
Coloring pages	/coloring.htm
Guidelines and rules	/rules.htm
Reading recommendations	/read_rec.htm

Though this may seem like an obvious thing to do, developers will often apply their own naming conventions to a site or use the default page names that a development tool provides. That approach works fine for the individual developer but can lead to confusion when the developer is no longer working on the project or is not available to make necessary changes. Trying to figure out where information is located and what files are called can be frustrating and time consuming, especially if the site contains a lot of scripting and include (.inc) files. Outlining some basic naming conventions as part of the storyboarding process can save a lot of headaches in the future.

Laying out the Screens

The final step in developing a storyboard for your site is perhaps the most creative and the most akin to the film industry's version of a storyboard. As you map the site, you begin to mock up and sketch what the screens will actually look like, much as film creators do when they draw out sequences for their camera shots. This allows you to see what your users will see on the screen as they travel through the pages of your site.

Storyboards need not be pretty and they need not be perfect. Rather, their purpose is to provide developers and project team members with a visual representation of the layout of the pages within your site. Your storyboards can be anything from rough sketches on sheets of paper to mock-ups created with software such as MS PowerPoint or Paint. The developer or designer who is building your site often creates the storyboards, but the task can actually be done by anyone and is a valuable exercise to have other project team members involved in.

As storyboarding progresses, you can easily see what navigational elements you will need to add to your site, how users will encounter information on the page, and what the elements on the screen will look like. Often through this process you will begin to notice where components are missing and where the content is so detailed that you need to expand the site. Here are some tips for creating storyboards:

Begin by sketching the components of your home page. Be sure to include the navigation elements (such as buttons and hyperlinks) as well as all key content and visual elements.

Keep your project plan, organizational charts, and flowcharts handy and refer to them when sketching layouts. Always keep in mind who your target audience is and what will appeal to them.

When sketching pages for a particular section, work through the screen layouts in the same way that children will use them. Complete the full sequence of screens before moving on to the next.

Give a title to each page (along with its file name) and provide a brief description of its content.

Aim for consistency from screen to screen, and make sure that the navigation structure lets users know where they are within the site. Keep in mind that many people may be entering your site from pages other than your home page.

Refer often to the content, navigation, and multimedia guidelines suggested in chapter 3.

Figure 6-5 shows PowerPoint-created storyboards for some secondary-level pages of the Public Library of Charlotte and Mecklenburg County's pre-opening ImaginOn site (http://www.imaginon.org). ImaginOn is the library's children's facility that will open in fall of 2005.

The creation of storyboards is an excellent exercise in developing screen composition and visual layout. Ideally, if your site is completely storyboarded, anyone should be able to look at your storyboards, no matter how crude, and put together the same website you or another web developer would have created. All three elements of a website's storyboarding

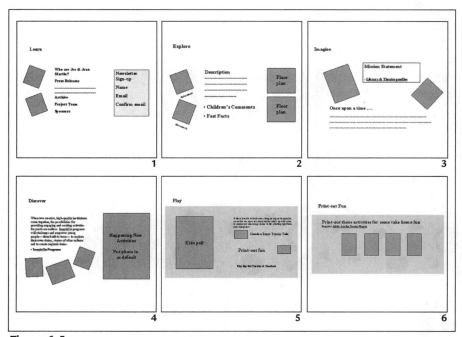

Figure 6-5
PowerPoint-Created Storyboard Pages for the ImaginOn Site

process are important to the overall design of the project. The organizational chart or flowchart helps to communicate the structure of the site, the naming conventions help to communicate the navigational protocols for the site, and the screen layouts communicate the look and feel of the pages within the site. Taken together, all three elements help web developers and graphic designers see your site as your project team envisions it and serve as the cornerstones of the web-development process.

NOTES

1. MindTools, "Brainstorming—Generating Many Radical Ideas," http://www.mindtools.com/pages/article/newCT_04.htm (accessed August 1, 2003).
2. Tony Tallent, Youth Services Coordinator, Public Library of Charlotte and Mecklenburg County, Charlotte, NC.

CHAPTER 7

Testing and Evaluation

When done right, testing and evaluation is more than a procedure performed at the end of a website's development cycle; it is an integral part of the entire development process. From the moment you first conceive the idea for your new children's service, you should begin testing it with your users. Will users find the idea of value? What site features will users find most appealing? If you involve your users throughout the concept design and development phases, you will establish a solid foundation that will serve you well when it is time to test the functionality and usability of your site.

FUNCTIONAL TESTING

Often when people think of website testing, they think only of usability testing, which is the process of testing a website's usefulness, effectiveness, and level of user satisfaction. In fact, usability testing is so important to the web development process that it now supports an entire industry. However, there is a whole area of functional testing that must occur before you can dive into examining the usefulness of a website. We will discuss usability testing later in the chapter, but first we will explore some of the functional aspects of a website that should be tested, including

Code validation

Hyperlinks

Performance

Browser compatibility

Screen adaptability

Accessibility

Since most of those components are tangible and their testing does not require a user to interact with the website, they can be easily evaluated using some type of testing tool.

Code Validation

There is nothing more annoying to a website user than missing images, unreadable characters, or markup language errors, and there is nothing more embarrassing to an organization than launching a site that contains such defects. During the development of a site, errors are unavoidable. Even the best web developers make programming and coding mistakes. The trick is to catch such errors through internal testing before they reach your users.

Checking by hand for HTML, scripting, and other coding errors can be tedious and take hundreds of hours, but mistakes can still slip through. Thus, checking for coding errors is best accomplished through validation checkers, many of which are now built into the web authoring tools that developers use. However, even if your web developer has used such an authoring tool, you may choose to run your site through a few validation checkers on your own, just to make sure no unnecessary errors can be found. There are a number of free as well as fee-based services that can assist you with this task. The World Wide Web Consortium (W3C), the governing authority of web standards, provides free access to two important and very useful validators:

Markup Validator (http://validator.w3.org), which checks HTML, XHTML, MathML and SVG markup languages

CSS Validator (http://jigsaw.w3.org/css-validator), which checks markup for cascading style sheets

Both tools are designed to locate and highlight where your code varies or does not fully comply with web standards. Because many different browsers and versions of browsers are in use and because some browsers are more forgiving of broken or sloppy code than others, it is important to use a good validation checker to catch the little oversights that you or your web developer might have missed.

Checking Links

Broken or missing hyperlinks will also drive users away from otherwise valuable websites. Such problems frequently creep in during the development process. File and directory names can change, and pages can be moved around, combined, or altogether deleted throughout the normal course of pulling a site's content together. Checking hyperlinks on a larger site that contains many internal and external links can be a cumbersome job for anyone. Fortunately, just like validation tools, there are plenty of link-checking tools available to assist you with this task. Many of today's web editing tools allow developers to check not only relative and page anchor links within a site but also external links, and will generate a report documenting the status of all the links found. On one hand, this report provides good insight into the amount of interaction and cross-referencing your site contains. On the other hand, it shows just how vulnerable the usefulness of your site might be to outside influences. The more links you have to external resources, the greater your need to develop a link-checking maintenance plan (see chapter 4). The W3C provides a valuable free tool that not only checks for broken links but also indicates which hyperlinks may pose a problem for some users in select browsers, such as hyperlinks generated through JavaScript:

> Link Validator (http://validator.w3.org/checklink), which checks hyperlinks (internal and external) and anchors within a website, and allows users to specify the depth at which the tool will scan through a site

Be sure to incorporate the testing of hyperlinks not only during the development and testing phases on your children's website but also as a part of the site's ongoing maintenance. Given the ever-changing nature of the Internet, websites change names and locations and come and go like the wind. What is a valid link today may not be tomorrow. Therefore it is best to incorporate link validation into your site's regularly planned maintenance routine.

Performance Testing

When you test the performance of your website, you are trying to evaluate its performance characteristics, such as speed and download time. You want to know, for example, how long it will take users to download your home page, how many users your site can support simultaneously, and what your web server's usage threshold is.

One of the ways to test performance is to run your website through a performance-testing tool. This will help you see how fast your site loads on different computers at various connection speeds and how robust your server is in handling multiple requests at one time. Very few libraries have the testing tools necessary to examine a website's stress or load level because such testing requires software that simulates an environment in which thousands of online users hit a site at the same time. Although most libraries create sites mainly for their local users and therefore do not expect to be bombarded by thousands and thousands of user requests at any one time, it is important to test performance from a user's standpoint, especially when it comes to download and access times.

Most web developers tend to have the latest, greatest, and most powerful computers on the market and therefore rarely see or experience the potential performance inhibitors in their own designs. They have no way of knowing how long it takes the website to load on a first-generation Pentium computer using a 24 Kbps or 56 Kbps modem or what the loading times are for the images and other elements found on the site. Although it is helpful to ask members of your staff and even your users to test the site from their home computers, it is hard to quantify the results. What may be an acceptable waiting period for one user may be unacceptable for another. Additionally, performance may be affected by web traffic through an Internet provider and by other programs or processes that may be running on a user's computer. Such outside factors complicate testing and make it hard to evaluate actual website performance.

Fortunately there are tools you can use to evaluate a website's performance. If you want to perform a stress or load level test on your site and its server, you might want to take a look at Microsoft's Web Application Stress software (WAS) or any number of other external software performance tools available for purchase. To test the loading times of your site, there are a few free website tools available. A useful one is

Website Tune Up (http://www.netmechanic.com/cobrands/zd_dev), created by NetMechanic in conjunction with ZDNet Developer, which will run several diagnostics on up to five pages for free and will include a report of measurable download times for connection speeds ranging from 14.4 Kbps to a T1 line (For a minimal charge you can upgrade to a version that will run more than five pages.)

A good performance goal is to keep page download time below 12 seconds for a 28.8 Kbps modem. If downloads take any longer, users are unlikely to stay around to see what your site has to offer. Although more and more people are switching to cable, DSL, and other faster Internet connections, you should not assume that all of your potential users are doing so. When it comes to attracting users, a site's download time is almost as important as the look and feel of its design.

Browser Compatibility

Any good web developer knows that all Internet browsers are not alike. What may look beautiful in the latest version of Internet Explorer may be an eyesore in another browser, such as Netscape. The differences can often be attributed to the browsers' developers, who have in the past frequently used proprietary tags that work properly only in their own platforms and that have not been officially adopted by the W3C. This problem is often exacerbated by the many web-authoring tools that favor one browser or another, such as Microsoft's FrontPage, which is biased toward Microsoft's Internet Explorer.

The best way around such problems is to see for yourself how your site will look in a variety of platforms. But unless your library has a wide range of PCs and Macs that are loaded with various versions of various browsers (Internet Explorer, Netscape, America Online, and the like), that may be impossible. Since most libraries' hardware and software are not on the cutting edge, the likelihood of your being able to manually test your website across all common browser platforms and configurations is low. If you have older browsers and computers at your disposal, you should definitely take advantage of them to test how your site performs. However, visually checking the compatibility of your site on one or two older platforms will not suffice; you need to be absolutely sure that your site will display well on *all* commonly used browser platforms.

There are several tools that will allow you to check the cross-browser compatibility of your site. One is NetMechanic's HTML Toolbox, mentioned previously, which evaluates how compatible your site is in the last three versions of Internet Explorer and Netscape Navigator. Another is

> BrowserCam (http://www.browsercam.com), which is a very reasonably priced tool, not only evaluates the compatibility of your site in six different browsers (including AOL) and three different operating systems but also provides screen captures of how your site actually looks in each of them; for $10 you can run 10 different URLs through their paces

Checking for compatibility issues up front can save you lots of time and energy later. Nothing is more disconcerting than listening to users complain that they are unable to view your site on their computers. And trying to resolve compatibility issues long after your web developer has moved on to other projects can be a nightmare. Using just a few simple tools to test the compatibility of your site will go far in ensuring that your site is usable for all.

Screen Adaptability

One of the early decisions that your team will have to make is what screen resolution your website will use. Today, the great majority of websites are designed for optimal viewing at a minimum resolution of 600 × 800 pixels. However, that does not mean that you should not test the look of your site at different resolutions. A site that looks wonderful in 600 × 800 may look awkward and off-center at higher resolutions if your developer has not designed it to remain centered on the page. And viewing the site at the lower resolution of 640 × 480 will show how much a user has to scroll to locate valuable information. With proper planning and design, users should not have to scroll to the fringes of your site to find its most valuable information; they should be able to see it easily within the viewable area of a smaller screen.

To test your site's screen adaptability, you should be able to use any computer that has a newer monitor. Today, most monitors can easily be adjusted to various screen resolutions right from the computer's desktop by accessing Display Properties. However, if you are viewing your site from a computer that has an older monitor or that has been locked down to prevent library patrons from tampering with its configuration, you might want to take a look at

Gdezigns Screen Size Tester (http://www.gdezigns.com/ScreenTester
.cfm), which is a free tool that shows how a page will look at screen
resolutions from 640 × 480 pixels to 1024 × 768 pixels

Accessibility

Accessibility testing ensures that the content on your website will be fully
accessible to all users regardless of physical abilities. Given that more than
10 percent of the online population is classified as disabled (750 million
people worldwide, 55 million Americans),[1] accessibility testing is not something to be taken lightly. In chapter 4, we presented guidelines for making
your site accessible to everyone. Ideally, those guidelines will be incorporated into your website's design from the very start. If they are not, you will
need to allow extra time at the end of your project to retrofit your site for
users with disabilities.

MANUAL TESTING

Although time-consuming to do, manually testing the accessibility of your
site enables you to view your site from the perspective of an individual with
disabilities. If you are lucky, your library system may offer patrons some of
the more common adaptive and assistive technologies (such as screen readers, alternative pointing devices, and screen magnifiers), which you can use
in your testing. But if not, Sue Bolander, a certified master HTML programmer, has outlined five simple steps you can take to test if your site is
accessible.[2]

Step 1: Turn off the Graphics

Use your browser's image setting to turn off the graphics on your site. To
do this in Internet Explorer, select *Tools* from the menu bar, then *Internet
Options*, and then *Advanced*. Look in the *Multimedia* section and remove
the checkmark from the option that reads "Show pictures." Once these
changes have been made, simply refresh your screen and you should be
able to view your site without images.

Are you able to understand the site without images? Can you navigate
around the site or to another page within it without visual clues? If not,
then you need to go back and reword the ALT tags of your images. These
alternative tags in HTML provide screen readers with textual descriptions
for the graphic elements that people with visual impairments are unable to
see. The use of ALT tags in your code is a WAI Priority Level 1 compli-

ance checkpoint. Without meaningful text in these tags, your site will be impossible for some users to use.

Step 2: Copy Your Site into Notepad

To view the contents of your page in linearized format—the same way many screen reader software programs read it to a visually impaired person—simply copy all the viewable contents of the web page into Notepad. To do this, use the *Edit* command from the browser menu and then click on *Select All* and then *Copy*. Next, open up Notepad and paste the copied text into it. You are now seeing the page the same way many screen readers would read the contents to a visually impaired person. Is some of the content of the site out of order, or is the text scrambled? If the page doesn't make sense, then you may need to examine the layout of your page to see what changes you can make to its structure so that the text falls into the correct sequence when linearized. More often than not this problem is caused by the incorrect use of tables and frames in your site's layout.

Step 3: View Your Site in Black and White

Print the pages of your site in black and white to make sure everything on it can be interpreted correctly without any color indicators present. Is there enough contrast to make the text legible against the site's background? If not, then you will need to adjust your screen and text colors so that information is clear and legible. Make sure none of your instructions on the site rely on color, such as "Use the green arrow to proceed." Also check your navigation structure to make sure all elements are viewable without the use of color.

Step 4: View Your Site without Its Style Sheet

The use of style sheets helps control the look and display of text elements within your site. If you temporarily remove or rename your style sheet and then refresh your page you will be able to view the text on the page without any defined font types, colors, or special formatting features. Does the text on your page look dramatically different? It should, but the page should still be functional. Can you alter the viewable text size using your web browser? (In Internet Explorer, select *View* from the menu bar and then *Text Size*.) If not, then the page's HTML probably contains hard-coded FONT tags, which may make the site impossible for a visually impaired person to use. To correct the problem, remove any FONT tags from the HTML found in the body of the page and use an external style sheet to control the text formatting.

Step 5: Unplug Your Mouse
When you unplug this all-too-familiar pointing device, you will force your-self into using the keyboard commands (Tab, Arrow, and Enter keys) to navigate your site. Can you maneuver around your site with just your key-board? Can you still use your forms? If not, then you'll want to examine the design of your page to see if any elements can be redesigned so that mobility around the site is improved and not dependent upon only a pointing device.

When you combine the preceding five simple tests you in effect do almost everything that software designed to review for accessibility does, with one large distinction. The manual method of testing focuses on enabling you to see your site much as someone with a disability might expe-rience it. Accessibility software, in contrast, focuses on reviewing the web pages' code for deviations from web accessibility compliance standards. Both methods have their merits and, when used together, they allow you to fully evaluate your site for any accessibility issues.

ACCESSIBILITY TESTING SOFTWARE

Several accessibility software products are on the market, but the most widely known and used is Watchfire's Bobby software (http://www.bobby .watchfire.com). Initially developed by the Center for Applied Special Technologies (CAST), Bobby is designed to expose potential accessibility compliance problems within a web page. It allows you to test for compli-ance using either the web content accessibility guidelines outlined by the W3C's Web Access Initiative or the government's Section 508 guidelines. Bobby's detailed reports identify where the elements of a website may need adjustment or correction in order to adhere to standard accessibility guide-lines. Bobby even organizes the report using WAI's three-level-priority checkpoint system, so that users can focus on Priority 1 issues before mov-ing on to others.

Figure 7-1 shows how Bobby software scans a web page and identifies the potential errors. The question marks on the page itself indicate only that some elements need to be carefully reviewed for compliance with accessibility guidelines, not necessarily that errors are present. Careful review of the detailed report that Bobby provides is necessary to determine whether a flagged item needs correction or not.

Although Bobby software does an excellent job of pointing out areas within a page's code and structure that may need correction, the results and

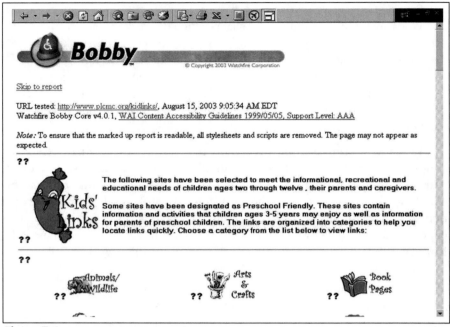

Figure 7-1
Sample Web Page Scanned by Bobby Software

recommendations in a Bobby report should be reviewed with caution. According to "How to Read the Bobby Online Report," a long report does not necessarily mean that a site has significant problems.[3] Experience and knowledge of accessibility guidelines and specifications are needed to apply the report results properly. Also, due to Bobby's inability to detect certain items, some flags will remain in the report after the corresponding issues have been corrected. Consequently, merely running your site through Bobby will not suffice; you also need to familiarize yourself with the accessibility guidelines.

The best way to test your site for potential accessibility issues is to combine manual evaluation with software testing. Each approach has distinct advantages, and when the two are used together, they provide a full set of tools that will enable you to ensure that your children's website will be accessible to everyone.

USABILITY TESTING

It may be hard to believe, but just less than a decade ago, the term "usability testing" barely existed in the world of web development. In fact, we can remember the first time that we used the term in our library, way back in 1998, when we conducted our first usability test with patrons. The initial question that many staff asked was, "What exactly is it?" Today, usability testing is one of the hottest topics in web development, and for good reason. The early 1990s were boom years for the Internet and the World Wide Web, and everyone, including public libraries, was jumping on the bandwagon in hopes of striking the information gold mine. For users in general, the Internet has indeed become a gold mine of information, but for information providers, the developers of the websites themselves, striking it rich on the Internet has become a larger struggle. In the decade or so since the global information network was born, website developers have quickly learned that it does not matter how much content your site may provide or how glossy its interface may be, if a site is not intuitive and easy to use, you will never get your users past its home page.

Usability testing measures the effectiveness, the efficiency, and the satisfaction with which users can achieve a set of tasks in a particular environment. This method of evaluation makes use of observed behaviors and feedback from test participants who work through problems in an effort to test the effectiveness and usefulness of a website. In a typical usability test, participants—one at a time or two working together—use a website to perform a specific set of tasks while one or more observers watch, listen, and take notes. The results are analyzed to establish the site's usability and to determine if design improvements need to be made.

Creating the Plan

Similar to the web development process itself, the planning stage of usability testing can be more involved than it would appear on the surface. In addition to identifying the elements of your site that you want to test, you also need to think about test script preparation, participants, location, equipment, logistics, and objectives.

TESTING OBJECTIVES

Establishing the goal and objectives for conducting a usability test is the first task your project team must undertake when preparing for usability testing. You need to identify both the overall goal of your usability test and the key areas or elements within the site for which you need user feedback. Pay particular attention to features that are new or dramatically different from other website services your library currently offers and on elements that you are most unsure or worried about. Such an approach will help you form your objectives and compile a list of elements that you need to test.

Some people think that usability testing is done only when you redesign an existing site, after you have a set of known problems that you want to correct. But that assumption is wrong. Granted, establishing usability test objectives is easier when you have an existing set of issues or problems that need to be addressed. However, it can be easily argued that those issues would not even exist if you had performed usability testing to begin with.

When developing objectives for testing a new website's usability, use the objectives from your original project plan. If one of the objectives in your project plan was to provide children with quality homework help resources, test your site's success in providing those resources. If an objective was to provide children with an online tool that allows them to recommend books they like to other children, develop a task that tests the achievement of that objective. Obviously, it would not make sense to develop your site for one set of objectives and then to test your site's usability based on a different set of objectives.

TEST SCENARIOS

A traditional usability test consists of a set of written tasks, or scenarios, that users perform when participating in the test. Often participants are asked to read a task out loud and try to complete it while observers watch and record their actions. The goal of such an approach is to ensure that all participants receive the exact same set of instructions. However, that method may not be particularly effective when the participants are children. Children's informational needs vary, and some children may need additional or different instructions in order to understand and perform the required tasks.

There are two different approaches you can use to develop questions for usability tests. When working with children, the best approach is to ask them directly to complete a task by saying, for example, "Please show me how you would use the website to find an article about our solar system." Children perform best when testing questions relate to real-world situations that they might encounter or tasks that they might be asked to do. In contrast, adults will often respond better to scenarios that ask them to assume the user role when working through a task. Therefore when developing the usability test for your children's website, you might want to consider defining each task using both a direct request and a role-playing scenario:

> Direct request for child: Please show me where to go on the website to find information about ancient Egypt.
>
> Scenario for adult: Your child has come to you for assistance with a homework assignment that asks him or her to use the library's website to locate information about ancient Egypt. Please show me where on the website you would take your child to find information about ancient Egypt.

In essence, both approaches ask the participant to complete the same task. However, the scenario for adults personalizes the task and makes test participants feel more comfortable about trying to work through the problem.

When developing a usability test, do not ask participants to answer too many questions or perform too many tasks. A good rule of thumb is to limit the number of testing questions (or scenarios) to no more than five or six. If you have too many scenarios to work through, your participants will become increasingly reluctant and the quality of their responses may suffer. Be sure to focus your questions on the most important objectives of your site. If the main objective of your website is to provide children with a tool they can use to record their favorite books, the most important thing to test is whether children can indeed use the site to record a favorite book. Make your tasks meaningful and significant to your project's main goal, and skip its superfluous content.

In their book *Usability Testing for Library Web Sites,* Elaina Nolan and CM! Winters recommend including two additional questions in your usability test:[4]

> What two things helped you the most when using this website?
>
> What two things need improvement to help you use this site better?

In most cases, testing participants will give you feedback continuously as they work through the tasks. However, there may be other elements of the site that they find confusing or have ideas about. Saving the preceding two questions for last allows participants to share their overall perceptions of the site, both what they like and what they dislike. The resulting dialogue may sometimes provide you with more useful information than you had bargained for. Be sure to take all suggestions and feedback in stride. You never know when a user will suggest a really outstanding idea that would never have occurred to you and that will lead to a new set of future enhancements.

Be sure to write all test scenarios down in a test script, and make sure that the test facilitators use the script. This will help to ensure that all test participants receive the same set of instructions. Do not allow the facilitators to ad-lib scenarios, because departures from the script will cloud your evaluation results. Even the smallest difference in how a task question is phrased can cause a huge difference in how a participant views and responds to the question. Consider the following two variations:

> Ad-libbed scenario 1: Imagine that you have just found a review of your favorite book on this website and you notice that some book reviews are accompanied by user comments. How would you add comments about your favorite book?

> Ad-libbed scenario 2: Imagine that you have just found a review of your favorite book on this website. Where would you go to add comments about it?

Both scenarios deal with adding user comments to book reviews found in a site. However, the first question asks users *how* they would go about completing the task, whereas the second question asks only *where* they would go to complete the task. Having the scenarios scripted and read to the participants will ensure that all receive the same set of instructions.

TESTING INSTRUCTIONS

In addition to writing out your test scenarios or questions, you will want to script a few general instructions or guidelines that will help test participants feel comfortable with the process. Your instructions should address the following questions that participants are liable to ask:

> How long will the test take?

> How many questions will you be asking me?

> Why do I have to think out loud?

> Who are the other people in the room? What will they be doing?

> What types of questions am I allowed to ask?

Here is an example of a scripted set of instructions:

> Thank you for agreeing to help us test our new children's website. During this test we will be asking you to imagine yourself in five different settings

while you work through tasks on the website. As you work through a task, we ask you to think out loud so that our observers can follow your train of thought. Please don't feel foolish about giving voice to what you're thinking; we ask everyone to do this. You are allowed to ask questions, but only of me. I may or may not be able to answer your questions, depending upon what they are. However, if you find that you can't figure out a task, just tell me. It's the only way we will know that we've made an important error in our website's design.

This evaluation process should take you approximately 10 to 15 minutes to complete. We will be happy to answer any of your questions about the testing process after we have gone through all five scenarios.

Sharing these instructions with your participants up front will help set them at ease with your usability testing process. In addition, Nolan and Winters suggest including a disclaimer in your testing script that not only helps to ease test participants' anxiety but also reminds test facilitators and observers about the purpose of usability testing:

Remember, the website and its design are what is being tested, not the person.[5]

Selecting Participants

There are three different types of participants in a formalized usability-testing process:

1. End users: users who participate in completing tasks and testing the site
2. Observers: participants whose sole responsibility is to observe and record end users' interaction and behaviors
3. Facilitator: the person who moderates or facilitates the testing process

The end users play by far the most important role in usability testing. However, without a facilitator to guide the testing process and one or two observers to record the results, usability testing would be worthless and nothing more than an exercise of blind discovery. To ensure that the results will be valuable in evaluating the site, all participants in a usability test must understand their roles.

END USERS

When selecting participants to test your website's usability, make sure to select members of your target audience. If your site is primarily targeted to children, you will want to have children well represented in your usability test. This does not mean that all your test participants should be children. As stated in chapter 3, the younger your website's primary audience is, the more adults your site is likely to have as a secondary audience. Therefore, among your test participants you will want to include not only children but also parents, caregivers, teachers, and anyone else who may be interested in what your new children's web service will have to offer.

It should be obvious that children who are too young to read or write are not the best candidates to participate in usability testing, even if your site is being developed with preschoolers in mind. Involving parents and caregivers of preschoolers as test participants makes much more sense, since they are the ones who will most likely be guiding their children's interaction with the site. Children who are able to read and write may be included as testers as long as they understand what the testing procedure is all about.

You can use a variety of methods to recruit test participants. One way is to quietly solicit the participation of some of your more frequent library patrons (children and adults) who you know represent the audiences that you are trying to reach. Most of these patrons will be delighted to assist you and will be interested in seeing what new and exciting things your library is cooking up. Another approach that we have found helpful is to post signs around the library asking for volunteers. For example:

WE NEED YOUR HELP!

The library is currently recruiting participants to assist us with evaluating a new children's website that we have developed. If you are interested in assisting us with a 10- to 15-minute exercise, please see a member of the children's services staff.

You might want to sweeten the pot by offering a fine-waiver coupon, free rental of a best-selling book, free library merchandise, or any other type of thank-you gift your library may be able to provide.

The importance of the role that the end user plays in ensuring the success of your new web service cannot be overstated. Without user input and assistance in testing the site's design, you cannot be completely confident that your new service will meet users' expectations and needs. End users' participation in usability testing enables you to revisit elements of your design that may be confusing or need refinement before you introduce your newest library service.

OBSERVERS

The role of the observer in usability testing is to study and record the behavior of test participants. Since this can be a difficult task, more than one observer is sometimes needed to record all the observations and end-user comments. After a test session has been completed, it is the responsibility of the observers to summarize their records and compare them with the facilitator's observations. During the test itself, the observers should remain as neutral as possible and should neither speak nor use nonverbal cues to communicate with each other or the test participant. Even though the observers may be out of view, sitting behind the end user, you do not want to run the risk that their presence will accidentally skew the test results. Some test participants may feel uncomfortable with so many people watching their every move, so the observers should try to alleviate as much awkwardness as possible by introducing themselves to each end user before the test begins.

FACILITATORS

The facilitator's main role in usability testing is to ensure that the end user is as comfortable as possible throughout the testing session. The facilitator needs to walk a fine line to put the participant at ease without providing too much assistance. Facilitators need to resist the urge to come to the rescue of participants who may be stymied by the task at hand. This can be especially hard for librarians, whose natural and professional inclination is to assist members of the public with finding information. However, if the facilitator gives too much assistance or reassurance, the recorded results will be skewed and unusable. Testing facilitators should keep the following tips in mind:

Try to distance yourself from the website during a usability test and keep an open mind. Try not to be drawn into a conversation in which you find yourself explaining the rationale behind something on the site.

Keep the participant talking out loud. This will allow you and the test observers to see where the user's logic and the website's design are leading. Since talking out loud, especially in a library setting (even behind closed doors), is not a natural behavior, you may need to gently encourage the participant several times.

Be naturally inquisitive and know when to jump in and ask questions. Sometimes an end user might make vague comments or suggestions that need more clarification. Do not feel shy about asking the person to explain what he or she means. Asking for clarification not only helps you better understand the user's thought process but also helps the user feel a little more comfortable with the process.

Offer participants encouragement as they work through the tasks. If participants become frustrated, gently remind them that they are not the ones being tested, the site is. Users should not be made to feel stupid if they do not understand a task or cannot complete it.

If a test participant asks you a direct question about the site, answer with a question. Example: User: "What does this text mean?" Facilitator: "What do you think it means?" This way, you will avoid being pulled into explaining the site and will refocus the user's attention back on the task. It is important to acknowledge the user's question in some way so that he or she will not feel ignored.

Above all, remember to respect all participants' feedback—good and bad. After all, how can you expect to develop a website that appeals to your target market if you fail to listen to and respect their concerns? Value your end users' opinions and be sure to thank them for their time.

Conducting the Test

Conducting a usability test can require a great deal of coordination and effort. A comfortable testing room needs to be reserved, equipment set up, staff shuffled around to cover desk scheduling, participants contacted, and testing arranged. One effective approach is to block out a full day and arrange your regular staffing so that the observers and the facilitator can be available without interruption.

HOW MANY PARTICIPANTS?

To facilitate participation in your test, consider scheduling your sessions around your library's story-hour time slots or other times when patrons are likely to be visiting and using your library anyway. If you find yourself without enough participants, do not hesitate to comb your book aisles or computer stations for the right volunteers. It is your responsibility to make sure you have a good sample of participants to assist with testing.

Usability guides suggest that you conduct tests with approximately five to seven users from your site's target audience. If your target audience is made up of two or more user groups (such as adults and children), you will want to test with three or four participants from each group. In fact, studies show that over 80 percent of a site's usability problems will be uncovered with as few as five test participants.[6] For a children's site, you will probably want to include both children and adults, in which case a sample of eight to ten participants (50 percent children and 50 percent adults) should be sufficient to uncover most potential usability issues.

THE TESTING ENVIRONMENT

Finding a quiet, comfortable room to conduct your testing is important, especially in a library setting. But unless your library has study or community rooms with Internet access, this may be hard to do. Another option is to use a staff member's office or back-office space. Those areas are more likely to have network connections and computers already set up, thus saving you the hassle of dealing with equipment issues. The important thing in selecting your test environment is to make sure you have a quiet location, free of distractions and foot traffic, where test participants can feel comfortable talking out loud.

TESTING TIPS

Since usability testing is so crucial to the design and overall success of your site, you will want to make sure everything goes as smoothly as possible. Here are some tips to keep in mind:

Keep the test session short (under 15 minutes). If users get stuck, gently move on to the next scenario or question.

Keep users thinking aloud. Use open-ended prompts to encourage them: "What are you thinking?" "What are you looking for?" "What do you want to do?"

Do not deviate from your test script. When working with younger test participants, it is tempting to depart from the script. Children look to adults for guidance and may even repeatedly ask for help in completing a task. If this happens, simply move the child to the next question by saying, for example, "This question seems a little hard; let's try another question."

Include review time after every session. Build in five to ten minutes of review time after each testing session so that you can compare notes with the other observers in the room. What one person misses, another might see. Your pooled notes will be especially helpful when it comes to evaluating the test results.

Remember the purpose of usability testing. Remind yourself and your participants often that the purpose of the exercise is to *test the website, not the user.*

Evaluating the Results

Once all your testing is complete, it is time to analyze your results. If your testing sessions are like most, you will have a pretty good idea of the major flaws in your design long before your last participant leaves. By the time you complete your third user session, chances are you will have already identified over 50 percent of the usability issues that you will need to address. If your users do not seem to be uncovering any noticeable design flaws, you may want to change your approach and ask for more feedback on what they like and do not like about the site. Phrase your questions to elicit the specific information you need—for example, "How would you change the site's design to make it easier to use?" and "What elements seem to be missing that would be helpful for the site to contain?" Such open-end questions may generate some elements and issues that you had completely overlooked and, as a result, were not even testing for.

When evaluating results, do not place too much importance on the responses of any one user. Although one participant's behaviors may uncover the most compelling information about your design, placing too much emphasis on those behaviors may do more harm than good. Redesigning your site to accommodate one user will not improve its usability for the majority of users. Try to give equal weight to all users' test sessions so that the focus will be on improving usability for everyone.

As you examine your usability testing results, tackle each task separately. This will allow you to evaluate all the participants' behaviors and responses as a whole. Begin with the first scenario or question and review all the notes taken by observers. Look for patterns in the participants' behaviors and record your findings. For example:

Scenario 1 (locating an article on the solar system)

50%—4 of 8 users—had difficulty locating the correct area of the site to go to. Three of those participants were children who did not seem to understand the term "online resources," but after moving beyond that, they were able to find an article.

38%—3 of 8 users—successfully completed the task with no difficulties and were able to quickly locate where they needed to go.

12%—1 participant—was completely lost.

Finding: Improvement could be made by replacing "online resources" with another term. One child suggested "magazines" and another child suggested "find stuff." An adult user suggested "articles and encyclopedias."

Once you have recorded all your usability results and findings, you can take your report to your project team for review. It will probably be obvious to all team members which elements of your site need to be improved. However, some team members may find it difficult to view the results objectively since they may feel married to certain elements of the site's current design. If this occurs, remind yourself and the team that the needs of users should come first, even if it costs a bit of extra development time.

The importance of functional and usability testing (such as code validation, browser adaptability, and accessibility) cannot be overstated. Testing, to be done correctly, must be a continuous and ongoing process that extends from your initial design all the way through your site's implementation and ongoing maintenance. In reality, the success of your site can never be hindered by too much testing, only by too little.

NOTES

1. Watchfire, "Accessibility: Enabling Access to Your Business," http://www .watchfire.com/products/webxm/accessibilityxm.aspx (accessed January 19, 2004).
2. Sue Bolander, "Is Your Site Accessible? Five Simple Tests," Designnewz.com, July 10, 2003, http://www.designnewz.com/designnewz-2-20030710IsYourSiteAccessibleFiveSimpleTests.html (accessed January 19, 2004).

3. Watchfire, "How to Read the Bobby Online Report," http://bobby.watchfire .com/bobby/html/en/readreport.jsp (accessed January 8, 2004).

4. Elaina Nolan and CM! Winters, *Usability Testing for Library Web Sites* (Chicago: ALA Editions, 2002), 33.

5. Ibid., 37.

6. Jakob Nielsen, "Why You Only Need to Test with 5 Users," useit.com, March 19, 2000, http://useit.com/alertbox/20000319.html (accessed January 19, 2004).

CHAPTER 8

Promotion and Marketing

B y now everything is in place. You have developed a wonderful website with engaging bells and whistles and interesting content, and you have a plan to keep it going. Kids will love it! Well, they will love it as soon as they know about and see it. All that is left now is getting the word out. A new restaurant may have a delicious menu and a classy chef, but all the food will go to waste if no one makes reservations. The secret for both the new restaurant and your website is . . . promotion, promotion, and promotion.

Whenever a library offers a program or begins a new service, it faces the challenge of promotion and the question of how best to get the word out. A research study by Wiman and Meierhenry (1969)[1] found that people remember 10 percent of what they read, 20 percent of what they hear, 30 percent of what they see, and 50 percent of what they hear and see. This would suggest that a multimethod approach might work best to ensure that children and families will read, hear, and see information about your site. Start with a wish list (a spot on the *Oprah Winfrey Show* would be nice!), then choose the best ideas for an obtainable and workable promotional package.

Traditional marketing theory suggests that the resources allocated to a project be divided in half, 50 percent for development and 50 percent for publicity. Libraries generally do not have advertising budgets, so following that formula is impractical. However, that does not lessen the importance of promotion. It merely indicates that inexpensive—better yet, free—ways of informing children and families about your new web service must be found.

Promotion should not be a one-time-only effort. It needs to begin before a site goes live and should be refreshed at every possible opportunity. An event to officially launch a site is great, but it should be considered only one part of a promotional package. Promotion is more than just advertising in its various forms. There are elements of promotion that involve the development of the website itself, and once they are in place, they work quietly behind the scenes to make your site visible. Unique domains and meta tags are two site-based promotional possibilities.

HELPING YOUR SITE SELL ITSELF: WEB TRAFFIC TRICKS AND TIPS

The Domain Game

For the most part kids, like adults, rely heavily on search engines to locate websites that interest them. In some cases they may go directly to a site's address if they have heard it mentioned by a friend, on TV, or through other media. Once in front of a computer, they will often assume the site has a .com ending. After all, their thinking goes, the most entertaining kids' sites are always the dot-com ones. And although we might wish to argue otherwise, the fact is that many gaming and activity sites developed for children are commercial in nature. Because of this, it is highly recommended that a library purchase not only the .org domain ending for a new site it hopes to create but also the .com version and possibly other endings as well (such as .info and .net). Doing so will not only assist your young patrons in finding your site more easily but will also help you in branding and effectively marketing your site as a unique service.

A logical question might be why a library would want to purchase a separate domain name for a children's service site instead of placing it within the library's current website. In fact, the reasons are many.

First and foremost, remember that your target audience is children and that today's children are used to having information pushed to them or readily available at their fingertips. They are not inclined to think of their local public library as the first place to begin searching for information, if they do any type of searching for information at all. Therefore, to reach out to children through your library's website, it is important to design services that speak directly to them and that are not buried within the second- or third-level pages of your library's general information site. The argument can easily be made that if you are going to go to all the trouble of developing a unique site for kids, it makes sense to purchase a domain name that children can readily identify with. Many children's libraries take a similar approach to their physical settings by designing library environments that appeal to young users. For the $20 to $35 cost of a typical hardcover book, which may circulate only about seven times a year from your library, you can easily purchase a domain that reaches thousands of children each year. Other benefits to hosting your children's site under a separate domain name include the following:

> Children can more easily identify with fun, kid-oriented domain names and are more likely to remember them. Good examples are Kidspoint.org, BookHive.org, and StoryPlace.org. (Many of these sites have been purchased in their dot-com versions as well.)
>
> You have greater freedom to create a site design that will appeal specifically to children. There are no predefined design elements (such as navigation structures) that you have to work with or layout templates that you must adhere to.
>
> It is easier to market your site through search engines and indexes. Your site will be displayed more prominently by search engines because your kid-friendly content will be readily apparent at the top level of your site. As a result, children will be able to find your site more easily.
>
> Last—and perhaps more important—your site will be found and accessed by children around the world, not just by kids in your local area. There is no better way to enable a larger audience of children to benefit from your library's expertise without affecting local library users' access.

It is a win-win situation for all. Children can more easily access quality sites and resources created by libraries, and libraries can more easily reach out to kids through the channels that kids are comfortable with.

Some Internet marketing experts suggest that purchasing domain names in common misspellings will further assist users in locating your site. Although we are not totally convinced that this is necessary, it does underscore the importance of selecting site names that are not too confusing for young readers (or adults) to spell. If you cannot purchase your desired domain name in all the three common endings (.com, .org, and .net), do not panic. Just make sure that the sites with the domain endings you do not or cannot purchase are not inappropriate for children and other potential users and are not in direct conflict with your site's mission.

Our library learned this lesson the hard way when were developing our portal student homework site, Brarydog (http://www.brarydog.net). Originally the site was to be called by another name, and we had purchased the corresponding domain name with the .org ending. At the time, the .com version had been purchased by another individual but had not yet been developed into a website. When our site was almost ready to unveil, we found out that the .com version of the site's name had been turned into a pornographic site. Needless to say, that site did not present an image that we wanted our children's homework site to be associated with, and it was certainly not a site that we wanted children to find by accident if they typed in the wrong ending. As you can imagine, the unveiling of our almost completed library service was halted abruptly and we went back to the drawing board on a new name. Lesson learned.

Tags: Keys to Searching Success

Whether or not you decide to create a unique domain for your site, your HTML code should incorporate the means to make your site visible to search engines. Each search engine works differently, but all have a formula that ranks results by how often words appear in various sections of a web page, including the URL, title, text, and meta tags. Meta data located in the header section of the HTML code for your site is particularly important. Attention to detail there can improve how your website is viewed and ranked by popular search tools. Meta data, which is aimed primarily at search engines, serves as unobtrusive publicity by helping children discover your site while using keywords to search the Web.

TITLE TAG

The title tag is a required element that provides the title of your web page and offers a description of it. Search tools read title tag information as part of their search formula. Users will see that information as it appears in the top bar of the browser (not on the page itself). That title is what will display in an individual user's list of bookmarks or favorite links, so clarity in your title tag will help children get back to your site for repeated visits. Title tag information is also captured and displayed as the description whenever someone lists a hyperlink to your page on another site. That is a lot of responsibility for one little line of code to carry! The good news is that a title tag enables you to get a lot of mileage out of a few carefully planned words. A good title tag should provide a simple, accurate description of a page with enough unique descriptors to make it stand out from the competition. In many cases, it may be the same as the title displayed on the page itself. If your site has a unique name that distinguishes it from other sites, including the name of your library may also be helpful. Each page within a site may have a different title tag, which is important whether your children's site is part of your library's main site or has its own domain. The title tag takes on increased importance for searchability if meta tags are not used. Two children's websites that have well-constructed title tags are KidsLinQ and Cool Reads.

KidsLinQ (http://www.kidslinq.org/books), Queens Borough Public Library, Jamaica, New York

Title Tag

<title>Queens Library KidsLinQ - Find Books and More - Recommended Reading</title>

> Even though this site has its own domain, the title tag connects it to Queens Borough Public Library. A Google search for "Queens library books" produced a link to this page, which appeared third in the results list.

Cool Reads (http://www.bpl.on.ca/kids/reviews.htm), Burlington Public Library, Burlington, Ontario, Canada

Title Tag

<title>BPLKids' Book Reviews: Burlington Public Library, Burlington, Ontario, Canada</title>

> The page displays the "kids @ the Library" logo and the title "Cool Reads." The phrase "book reviews" is not displayed, even though it is the subject of the page. The title tag acts as a descriptor that expands what is viewed on the page. A Google search for "book reviews Burlington" lists this page first in its results.

Be descriptive with your title tags and do not worry about keeping them to a minimal number of words. It is recommended that title tags not exceed 100 characters so that the full title will appear in the browser's title bar. However, because title tags greatly influence your search engine ranking, you do your site a great disservice if you limit yourself to too few words.

META TAGS

Meta tags add more search power to your site by including keywords and phrases that children might use when searching. Not all search engines use meta tags, but including them cannot hurt. Unlike the information in title tags, the information in meta tags is for search purposes only and is not viewed by users. There are several types of meta tags, but the two we will focus on are description tags and keyword tags.

Description Tags

The description meta tag provides a basic description of your site. It supplements the information in the title tag and acts as a hidden annotation of your website. Different search tools use this information in different ways, from displaying it as the description in the results list to including it as part of a ranking formula. The Talking Tales site of the Calgary Public Library has an effective description meta tag.

Talking Tales (http://calgarypubliclibrary.com/kids/story/welcome .htm), Calgary Public Library, Calgary, Alberta, Canada

Description Meta Tag

<META NAME="description" CONTENT="Join us for a first in a series of online story-times.">

Keyword Tags

The keyword tag takes into consideration the various keywords or phrases that children and their families may use to conduct a search for a website. A keyword tag is an excellent place to include possible misspellings and words and phrases that are similar to those used in the title and description tags. Plural versions of terms are not needed. Both Potamus Place and Brarydog have well-thought-out keyword tags.

Potamus Place (http://www.potamusplace.net), Cleveland Heights–University Heights Public Library, Cleveland Heights, Ohio

Keyword Tag

<META NAME="Keywords" CONTENT="Kids, Potamus Place, Potamus Press, Cleveland Heights, Heights Library, public, library,

public library, libraries, books, magazines, resources, databases, research databases, videos, catalog, research, branches, reading, electronic resources, news, reference, children, adults, parents, literature, information, computers, Pathfinders, Know It Now, connect, homework, picture books, picture book search, games, secret games, summer reading, summer reading lists">

Brarydog (http://www.brarydog.net), Public Library of Charlotte and Mecklenburg County, Charlotte, North Carolina

Keyword Tag

<META NAME="keywords" CONTENT="brarydog, mylibrary, personalize, library portal, librarydog, encyclopedia, newspapers, Electric Library, magazines, Facts on file, almanacs, worldbook, homework assistance, brary dog, reference, news, Novelist, public library, bizlink, healthlink plus, encyclopedia americana, grolier, transcripts, reference USA, my library, plcmc, charlotte public library, blue dog, prarriedog, pr newswire, NCLive, StoryPlace, homework help, term papers, reports, bibliography, personal reference tool, Brary Dog, http://www.brarydog.net, http://www.brarydog.com, http://www.brarydog.org">

As you can see from the examples, a set format is used for meta tags:

<META {TAG}="type" CONTENT="description or keywords">

Words and phrases in the body of the tag are separated by commas. The symbol < signals the beginning of the tag, and the symbol > signals the end. Some developers prefer to write their own code, but tools are available that will compile tags from the basic information you provide.

Registering Your Site

It is never wise to leave things to chance. Good use of tags is wise, but getting registered with top search tools is even wiser. Directories such as Yahoo! compile suggested sites

---

FREE META TAG CREATION TOOLS

Meta Tag Builder (http://www.localsubmit.com/metatags.asp), by Local Submit

Meta Tags Generator (http://www.submitexpress.com/metatag.html), by Submit Express

Meta-Tag Generator (http://www.siteup.com/meta.html), by SiteUp Networks

and arrange them by category, and therefore do not randomly find sites. Search engines such as Alta Vista and Google use crawlers to search for the keywords used in a search, then assign relevancy to the results. Directories require registration because they display results only from selected sites. Various forms of registration with search engines may increase your ranking and improve your site's visibility. Here are a few tips about registering your site.

> Be selective. Choose a few top search engines and directories, paying attention to which are under the same umbrella. (For example, in March 2000, Yahoo! purchased Inktomi, which powers MSN, Altavista, Looksmart, and HotBot.)
>
> Do not pay. If a search engine or directory charges a fee, do not register with it.
>
> Be sure to register with children's search tools, such as Yahooligans! and Ask Jeeves for Kids.
>
> Do it yourself. It is not that time-consuming to find the submission requirements for your chosen search tools. Start at the search tool's home page. You might need to look around a little. For example, Yahoo! recently started a fee-based submission service, but the link to basic site suggestion is located at the bottom of the page. (Look for the link "How to suggest a site.")

BACKLINKS

Backlinks are links that lead from another website to your site. The more links to your site the better, so encourage backlinks from the beginning. State on your page that links to your site are welcome. If you have a preferred icon or wording to use in your site's reference, provide that in the "invitation to link" section. Backlinks can be tracked, so some interesting information about who is using your site can be gathered. An unintended audience, for example, may be revealed. Such is the case of PLCMC's StoryPlace site, which we were surprised to discover is widely used in Korea as a tool to learn English.

AWARDS PAGE

Once you receive recognition for your site, make sure to share your glory. A page presenting details about awards, positive reviews, and favorable quotations should be easily accessible to users. A link from the home page works well. Recognition adds authority to your site, so take the opportunity to brag a bit.

Once you have done everything possible to make your website easy to find on the Web, it is time to begin actively promoting it. This involves marketing your site both inside your library and externally throughout your community.

IN-LIBRARY PROMOTION

A good way to start promoting your new website is with children and families who already use the library. Think about how your library usually informs patrons about children's programs and services. Identify what is the same about promoting your website and what is different. Consider how your library home page is promoted. Determining what promotional methods already work best for your library and its patrons is a good start in developing a marketing plan. Once you have that information, you can consider new options that might work especially well to encourage Web traffic to your site.

Print Materials

Print promotional materials can be very effective. They can also be economical if you can incorporate them into regular library publications, such as monthly newsletters or announcements. Fliers can be created with a word processor and printed on colored paper for emphasis. If money is available for professional printing, you can create some glossy, eye-catching materials to encourage children to visit your new site.

FLIERS

Traditional half-sheet fliers with information about your website are simple to create and easy to distribute at a circulation or reference desk. Include any important facts about the site and, of course, the URL. If your site features a distinctive character or unique artwork, including it in the flier provides a visual connection. Consider offering a coupon that can be retrieved from the website by using a password that is revealed in the flier. The coupon (for a free library rental or credit toward library fines) could then be printed and redeemed.

BOOKMARKS

Who does not need a bookmark? Bookmarks are easy to create and inexpensive to print in-house or at a printer. Children can take bookmarks with them, use them, and be reminded of your website each time they read a book. There is little room on a bookmark for information, so keep your message concise and catchy. If your site will require users to set up an account, provide a place on the bookmark for children to write down their log-in information. Good distribution techniques are to include a bookmark in every children's book or to hand out at least one bookmark per child at checkout.

NEWSLETTERS

If your library puts out a monthly newsletter, include an article about your new site. Newsletters go out to huge mailing lists, and if people do not have children or grandchildren, they probably have friends who do. Spark readers' interest—tell them how to get to the site and what children will be able to do when they get there. Newsletters are for adults, so convince them that children will really want to visit and use your new online service.

Displays

The number of ways to display information at your library is limited only by your imagination. Do not write off the possibility of a display because you think there is no room. A half-sheet acrylic holder can display an attention-grabbing flier on even a crowded desk. Acrylic display holders come in various sizes and are easy to change. A poster mounted on foam core with a homemade stand can be placed on a desk or an easel. If such options still take up too much space in your library, hang a poster from the ceiling. A variety of poster holders are available from library materials vendors and printers. One that our library has used effectively creates a three-sided display mobile that can stand or hang and makes the information visible even if it spins. Take advantage of whatever space your library has to offer: bulletin boards, trade show displays (desktop versions are very inexpensive), covered display boards, or whiteboards. Any and all display methods can have an impact.

Wearable Promotions

Why not wear your message? T-shirts displaying a screen shot of your website and its URL are fun to wear and are great attention getters. Screen-printed shirts can be purchased, or if you need only a small number, consider making the shirts yourself with iron-on transfers. A favorite wearable item of ours is buttons. Create buttons using a button maker and have staff wear them, or use them as giveaways.

Library PCs

Your new children's service website can attract users from around the world, but do not forget the children visiting your library! It is great for children to use the site from home, and a good way to introduce them to the site is to make it accessible on computers in your children's area. At the library, they can not only use the site but also receive a guided tour of its features from the staff. A shortcut and unique icon on the computer's start menu will also help children find the site and remind them that it is available. Another nice publicity trick is to use an image from the site as PC wallpaper. As always, include the URL. Our library uses a montage of images from our different sites as a reminder to users every time they sit down at a library computer.

Electronic Newsletters

We previously mentioned printed newsletters, but many libraries now have separate e-mail newsletters. There may be some duplication between the two, but not all information is the same. E-mail newsletters need to be very brief to ensure that recipients will not delete them before getting your message, so a few intriguing sentences about your new service should suffice. If it is not already in your project or maintenance plan, think about having a newsletter about your site only. Such a newsletter does not have to go out monthly, but it is a great way to quickly let people know when updates and changes occur. Post an area on your site where users can sign up to receive these e-mail updates.

Programming

Programs that tie in with your website support the project and get more staff involved. For example, if your website has stories, you can show one at story time. If book reviews are a feature, have a book talk or author program and demonstrate how children can find reviews on your site or submit their own. Reviews can be written and collected during a program and then published on the site. Your imagination will provide the inspiration. Just think of how your site can be used with a group of children, and let the fun begin.

Giveaways

Giveaways can be great fun and have a variety of uses. Giveaways, which rarely have much printable space, should show at least the name of the site and its URL. Pencils are a great giveaway and are usually inexpensive. Our library has used poetry magnets, slider puzzles, screen wipes, and die-cut bookmarks to promote our children's sites. One of our most popular give-aways is a zipper pull in the shape of Brarydog. Buttons and notepads (printed with a color printer, cut with a paper cutter, and stapled together) are two examples of giveaway items that can be made inexpensively by the library.

Links on Library Websites

Whether your site stands alone or is a page within your library site, link to it from the library home page and any other page that makes sense. Keep it visible, and give children as many doorways to your site as possible. Try writing a trivia question about your site, with the correct answer linking to your page.

Staff

Library patrons and outside users may not be the only targets of your marketing efforts. You may also have to market your new site to staff. Since only a few people on your staff will have worked on the project, the rest will need to be educated about it so they can recommend it to patrons. E-mails, intranets, and branch/service-area meetings are all excellent ways to notify staff of your new website. Be sure to give staff an opportunity to see and play with the site before it goes live. If you get staff excited about the project, they will happily assist you in spreading the word.

Teaser Campaigns

A teaser campaign builds curiosity about a site before its actual launch. The Public Library of Charlotte and Mecklenburg County used this technique when it launched its student homework site, Brarydog. Giant footprint stickers with "www.brarydog.net" written on them appeared on all library floors, leading patrons to the PCs. Posters with Brarydog peeking out of his prairie dog hole were placed in all locations, and Brarydog appeared on billboards and in newspaper ads weeks before the site premiered. Developing a promotional package that teases the public and increases curiosity about the site is an excellent way to build excitement. A teaser campaign does not always require a big budget—you can also easily create one using bookmarks, posters, or announcements on your website. The possibilities are endless, and can be customized to fit what will work best for your library and its budget.

EXTERNAL PROMOTION

Media coverage is a fabulous form of external promotion, if you can get it. Be on the lookout for alternative means of letting the community know about your new service. Connect with other institutions that work with children, or woo businesses that might be willing to make donations to support and promote your site. The most likely avenues for free promotion are schools, local events, donations, electronic discussion lists, and professional journals.

Schools

What better place to reach children than at school? Schools can be great partners, and teachers and media specialists can be invaluable allies. Let teachers know how your site supports education and curriculum. Create a sample lesson plan around your site that teachers can easily incorporate into their curricula. If you highlight your site's relevance to the teachers' world, teachers will be more likely to recommend your site to their students.

Local Events

Find out which community events throughout the year invite not-for-profit organizations to participate. A booth can offer superb promotional opportunities. Supply bookmarks, fliers, and library card applications, and staff the booth with a person knowledgeable about the library in general, not just about your site. If possible, make a computer part of your booth display, so people can see the website firsthand. If you host your own site, it is possible to can the site so it can be viewed offline. When manning a booth, do not wait for people to ask you questions. Instead, ask them questions, such as "Are you familiar with our new website?" or "Would you like to listen to a story?" Taking the initiative will help you draw more interest in what your library has to offer, and we all know that libraries today offer far more than most people realize.

Since each event has its own personality and clientele, participating in multiple events will help you reach a wider variety of populations. Look for opportunities where you might not expect them, such as at a comic book convention, and be prepared to answer not only questions about your new library website but also general questions about the library itself.

Donations

Libraries are skilled at acquiring donations, so put that skill to work for you. Find out who would be willing to give ad space, billboard space, or promotional items such as pencils or bags. If there is a staff member responsible for marketing, ask him or her to help. Many businesses are on the lookout for methods to promote themselves as community- and family-friendly enterprises. You never know who might be willing to support the library by underwriting some of its marketing, and services for children have great appeal.

Electronic Discussion Lists and Professional Journals

Libraries love to share what they have done in hopes that other libraries can benefit from their experiences. Post information about your children's site on electronic discussion lists such as ALSC-L[2] and PUBYAC,[3] and submit articles to professional journals. Raising awareness of your site in these ways can promote backlinks to your site and provide helpful guidance to libraries considering similar projects. It can also generate valuable feedback.

In summary, promotion is the key to getting your site off the ground and keeping it highly visible to current and potential users. Good initial promotion, and a good website, will foster their own publicity as people link to your site and tell friends to visit it. Make promotion a permanent agenda item for your monthly team meetings, and compile a running list of promotional possibilities.

The key to creating an innovative children's web service lies not only within the site's functionality, creativity, and ability to appeal to and engage children but also within your library's ability to successfully market the site. Take advantage of any and all channels to promote your new service. If you constantly promote and market your innovative children's site to potential users, your library will never stop attracting young patrons.

NOTES

1. Raymond V. Wiman and Wesley C. Meierhenry, eds., *Educational Media: Theory into Practice* (Columbus, OH: Charles Merrill, 1969).
2. Subscription information available at http://www.ala.org/Content/NavigationMenu/ALSC/News6/Electronic_Discussion_Lists1/Electronic_Discussion_Lists.htm.
3. Subscription information available at http://liblists.wrlc.org/LiblistsQueries/TDetail.idc?LisID=235.

RFP for Hands on Crafts Children's Website

REQUEST FOR PROPOSAL
FOR WEAVING A TALE OF CRAFT PROJECT

Invitation for Proposals

A collaborative effort of the Public Library of Charlotte & Mecklenburg County (PLCMC), the Mint Museum of Art (MMA) and the Mint Museum of Craft + Design (MMC+D) seeks a qualified web designer/design firm to assist in the graphic development of an interactive web site for children.

Interested parties are asked to submit 3 copies of their proposal no later than 5:00 P.M. on March 15, 1999 to:

> Tale of Craft Project Coordinator
> Public Library of Charlotte & Mecklenburg County
> 310 N. Tryon Street Charlotte, NC 28202

Background

The Public Library of Charlotte & Mecklenburg County and the Mint Museum of Art have obtained a grant to design "Weaving a Tale of Craft Project" (WTCP), an innovative, educational program which includes (among other educational and program components) an interactive web site for children and families.

The primary objectives of this project are to:

- Build an appreciation for craft (ceramic and textile) and an in-depth understanding of its processes.

- Create a web site to compensate for the lack of printed resources about crafts for children and youth.
- Share North Carolina's rich cultural heritage of crafts.

The Web site produced should have a distinctive and consistent design and provide a template for the development of future pages. The Web site should be easily navigable by school-aged children and their families, as well as highly graphic rather than text laden.

As the keystone of this program, the web site must be interactive, informative, accessible and fun.

Scope of Work

- The focus of the web site will be ceramics & textiles (phase 1: ceramics).
- Utilize the MMA's existing audio and video clips about the creative process.
- Design of web page to include North Carolina's cultural heritage.
- Consistent imagery and use of interactive components with an intuitive navigational flow.

Once a designer/design firm has been selected in accordance with the procedures the WTCP and the designer shall develop a mutually agreed upon detailed scope of work which is to include a fixed price and a timeline for completion. Although the contracted work will not include the development of content, the selected designer will place content on the web within the provided framework.

Where desirable and technically feasible, the WTCP is interested in incorporating interactive features such as Macromedia Shockwave and Flash, including database connectivity on the web site.

Project Timeline

Grant specifications outlined the start date and completion of phase 1 by December 31, 1999. The designer/design firm and the coordinator will have no less than two reviews prior to the project's completion. A timeline will need to be worked out between the designer/design firm and WTCP in order to accommodate reviews and users testing within an appropriate window before the specified completion date.

Contents of Proposal

Proposals must include, but need not be limited to, the following information:

- Overview of qualifications.
- Samples of prior work may be submitted in hard copy; or the web address of pages designed.
- An estimated cost for the project (broken down into components if possible). Although the selected designer/design firm will ultimately be required to commit to a fixed (not to exceed price) please include a per hour fee for performing the type of services requested.
- Summary of your web development process and timeline for project.

Ownership of Work

All images, icons, designs, layout, drawings plans, databases, specifications, computer files and other materials created or developed pursuant to this RFP shall be the sole property of PLCMC. Designer may duplicate copies of such materials for their own files or for such other purposes as may be authorized in writing by the Project Coordinator.

Additional Information

See Preliminary Project Plan. (attached)

Reservations

The WTCP Directors and Coordinator reserve the right to reject any or all bids and any items therein, and to waive any non-conformity or proposals with the RPF, whether technical or substantive nature, as the interest of the program may require.

RFP Not Contractual

Nothing contained in the Request for Proposal shall create any contractual relationship between the proposer and PLCMC, MMA and MMC+D.

Thank you for your interest in this exciting endeavor.

REFERENCES

Braun, Linda W. *Teens.Library: Developing Internet Services for Young Adults.* Chicago: ALA, 2002.

Dowling, Thomas. *Library Web Manager's Handbook.* Chicago: ALA, 2003.

Fountes, Irene C., and Gay Su Pinnell. *Matching Books to Readers in a Balanced Literacy Program.* Portsmouth, NH: Heinemann, 1999.

Holmes, Merlyn. *Web Usability and Navigation: A Beginner's Guide.* New York: McGraw-Hill/Osborne, 2002.

Looney, Michael, and Peter Lyman. "Portals in Higher Education." *EDUCAUSE Review* 35, no. 4 (July/August 2000).

Lopuck, Lisa. *Web Design for Dummies.* New York: Hungry Minds, 2001.

Malone, T. W., and M. R. Lepper. "Making Learning Fun: A Taxonony of Intrinsic Motivation for Learning." In *Aptitude, Learning and Instruction,* edited by R. E. Snow and M. J. Farr. Vol. 3, *Cognitive and Affective Process Analysis.* Hillsdale, NJ: Lawrence Erlbaum, 1987.

Minkle, Walter, and Roxanne Hsu Gledman. *Delivering Web Reference Services to Young People.* Chicago: ALA, 1999.

Niederst, Jennifer. *Web Design in a Nutshell.* 2nd ed. Sebastopol, CA: O'Reilly, 2001.

Nielsen, Jakob, and Shuli Gilutz. *Usability of Websites for Children: 70 Design Guidelines.* Fremont, CA: Nielsen Norman Group, 2002. Available at http://www.nngroup.com/reports/kids.

Nolan, Elaina, and CM! Winters. *Usability Testing for Library Web Sites.* Chicago: ALA, 2002.

Walter, Virginia A. *Children and Libraries: Getting It Right.* Chicago: ALA, 2001.

Watchfire. "Web Accessibility." http://www.watchfire.com/products/webxm/accessibilityxm.aspx.

W3C. "Web Content Accessibility Guidelines 2.0." http://www.w3c.org/TR/2004/WD-WCA920-20040311.

Wiman, Raymond V., and Wesley C. Meierhenry, eds. *Educational Media: Theory into Practice.* Columbus, OH: Charles Merrill, 1969.

INDEX

Helene Blowers is currently the director of Web Services for the Public Library of Charlotte and Mecklenburg County (PLCMC) in North Carolina. Under her direction, PLCMC has become a nationally recognized leader for its unique Internet service sites for patrons. Among the most popular of these are the library's award-winning sites for children, StoryPlace (www.storyplace.org) and the BookHive (www.bookhive.org).

Robin Bryan is an information specialist for the Public Library of Charlotte and Mecklenburg County. She has worked as a children's specialist, as a help desk coordinator, and as the library's Brarydog coordinator, educating children and adults about the library's unique homework help web portal. She is the co-author of *E-Book Functionality: What Libraries and Their Patrons Want and Expect from Electronic Books* for LITA and of articles in *Public Libraries*.